lenparent

styleyoursenses

seersuckerandsaddles

krystalschlegel

mrscocowyse

simplytandya

dressupbuttercup

lifewithjazz

michelle_janeen

fashiioncarpet

heyitsyash

champagneandchanel

ellabrooksblog

onesmallblonde

jadorefashion

jaimeshrayber

LIKEtoKNOW.it

STORIES FROM THE INFLUENCER NEXT DOOR

Published by LIKEtoKNOW.it

Dallas, TX

www.liketoknow.it

Distributed by Greenleaf Book Group

For ordering information or special discounts for bulk purchases, please contact Greenleaf Book Group at PO Box 91869, Austin, TX 78709, 512.891.6100.

Design and composition by rewardStyle, Inc

Cover design by rewardStyle, Inc

All photographs provided by the influencers featured as part of their stories.

Photo credits can be found on page 232.

Publisher's Cataloging-in-Publication data is available.

Print ISBN: 978-0-692-14006-2

Part of the Tree Neutral® program, which offsets the number of trees consumed in the production and printing of this book by taking proactive steps, such as planting trees in direct proportion to the number of trees used: www.treeneutral.com

Printed in the United States of America on acid-free paper

18 19 20 21 22 23 24   10 9 8 7 6 5 4 3 2 1

First Edition

For influencers around the world, the current and future creative entrepreneurs: may you have the guts to launch and the grit to keep going.

CONTENTS

| influencer profiles you can find, follow, and shop in the LIKEtoKNOW.it app

◈VENZEDITS

Amber Venz Box

est. 2010 | Dallas, Texas

For as long as I can remember, I have wanted to work in the fashion industry. As an elementary school girl, I would call my best friend and tell her what to wear to school the next day so we could coordinate on the playground. In 5th grade, I was asked to leave math class because I was caught knitting and vending scarves in the back row of class, and in middle school, I had a denim business where I took vintage jeans and turned them into skirts. My freshman year of high school, I carried around a book filled with drawings of a clothing collection I had designed (called "VENZEL"), and later in college, I went on to launch my own jewelry line, became a retail buyer, and then a personal stylist.

In April of 2010, at the age of 22, I published a website, venzedits.com, where I documented my personal styling work. I posted three times daily—one outfit post, one trend story, and one sale find or frugal styling tip. I found out that my website was a "blog" when *The Dallas Morning News* ran a full-page article titled *Meet the Blogger*, announcing that the shopgirl and jewelry designer people knew from around town was now offering her personal shopping service for free, online.

I loved sharing my work and point of view online; it was so much more gratifying than working with just a single client each day. With the blog, I got to share ideas with anyone who was interested. I got to style photo shoots, learn to edit photos, and share my personal-style wins and secrets with people who cared about fashion the way I did—people who visited my site. During college, I applied several times to work as a summer "closet intern" at one of the biggest publications in New York, but my applications were never acknowledged. Having my own site allowed me to be the fashion editor I had always aspired to be. Being a blogger gave me the opportunity to create the career I had always wanted, in my city, on my terms.

In 2011, a year after I launched my blog, I was all-in on my new hobby, but I needed to find a way to earn a living. At that time, "blogging" was not a respected activity and it was certainly not a career choice.

Baxter, my then-boyfriend, now-husband, and I set out to find a solution that would allow me to turn my blogging hobby into my full-time job; so we created a tech platform that would ultimately empower me and my newfound peers—other bloggers like me—to become true digital entrepreneurs; the kind that could support ourselves and our families. rewardStyle launched that June.

Today, the rewardStyle team is made up of hundreds of employees who work from our offices across four continents and provide service in more than a dozen languages—from Shanghai to São Paulo, Dallas to London and Berlin, and New York to Los Angeles, this team wakes up every day with a single mission: to empower influencers to become successful entrepreneurs.

What started as an idea in a studio apartment in Dallas, Texas is now fueling an entirely new industry and powering the businesses of tens of thousands of creative entrepreneurs around the world.

In 2017, rewardStyle created and launched the LIKEtoKNOW.it app, and today, it is the largest contextual shopping app in the world; the millions of original images found in the app were all created and published by influencers and they are 100% shoppable. The LIKEtoKNOW.it app is a destination where you can discover people, looks, and products—all in context—and then curate them, and shop when you are ready.

As we built the company over the last seven years, I've met influencers from all over the world, in their hometowns, in their favorite restaurants and coffee shops, and in their homes. What is striking about these influencers is that they are all normal people, just like you and me. They come from all types of cities and countries and family types and their ages are as varied as their professional backgrounds. In the book, you will read about nurses, parents, chief architects, teachers, and even a high school student, all of whom decided to embark on building a business of their own. What these influencers have in common is that they are all entrepreneurs; they all had the guts to *launch* and the grit to keep going.

The LIKEtoKNOW.it app is a place where they share their world, just for you. They document their wardrobes, homes, vacations, family life, beauty and fitness routines, and more. Together, they have created a mobile universe that is completely shoppable, making the LIKEtoKNOW.it app a place for you to find your people and curate and your life.

There are more than 100 LIKEtoKNOW.it Influencers featured in this book, but there are tens of thousands of wildly successful influencers who have unique journeys that they share in the app every day and millions who are just embarking on this path. Together, these influencers have created a new industry—and a new way to look at careers and entrepreneurship—while providing us, their followers, with a new way of curating a beautiful life that is more convenient, accessible, authentic, and inviting than ever before.

In reading this book, I hope you find your people—the ones with backgrounds, circumstances, and dreams just like you—and that their stories empower you on your journey.

Gratefully,

Amber Venz Box
President & Co-founder, rewardStyle & LIKEtoKNOW.it

⊕ HAPPILYGREY

Mary Lawless Lee

est. 2012 | Nashville, Tennessee

What were you doing before you launched *Happily Grey*? I was a registered nurse working as a cardiovascular intensive care nurse. It was intense but incredibly rewarding.

What inspired you to become an influencer? When I started blogging, I was desperate for a creative outlet. My day job was literally life and death, and I needed a distraction. I've always been into both fashion and photography, so blogging was incredibly interesting to me.

Has your blog always been called *Happily Grey*? My blog is, and always has been, *Happily Grey*. I grew up in a pretty black and white world. While I appreciate the values that were instilled in me while I was young, life quickly taught me that living between the lines is more realistic. Flexibility is important. Life doesn't always have to be black and white, and often the best moments are those in the grey!

Did anyone help you start? Early on, there were a few bloggers I followed and admired that were open to sharing their approach and perspective. It was a great way to start out in the community; from a place of supporting each other instead of competing all the time. I also had a super talented friend, Michael Anderson, who built my website in his free time. He made it easy to get the look I wanted for less.

What is one of your favorite quotes that puts things into perspective for you? "Ya blew it!"

Silly, I know, but too often I get hyper-focused on deadlines and details and deliverables—it's good to be organized and driven, but no one is perfect! I mess things up all the time, and instead of carrying it with me into the next day or collaboration, I have to remember that it's important to have a sense of humor.

✷ CELLAJANEBLOG

Becky Hillyard

est. 2012 | Kansas City, Kansas

How did your digital brand get its name? My blog, *Cella Jane*, is named after my grandmother, Marcella Jane, who influenced my love for style.

How has being an influencer changed your life? It has changed our lives immensely. I never thought in a million years that I would have a thriving business that I not only love, but also provides for my family. My husband helps with the business daily and it has given us so many amazing opportunities that we are grateful for.

What advice would you give to those who want to follow in your footsteps? When I first started, I remember looking at top bloggers with admiration. I would often dream to be there someday, wondering if it was something I would be able to do. I want to inspire others and also offer reassurance that with hard work and lots of perseverance, you too can succeed and reach your goals. Whatever that may be, if you have that passion to make it happen, you really *can* do it!

My husband was able to quit his job and now helps me full time with the blog, and I love that this is an adventure we get to be on together.

✪LAURENKAYSIMS

Lauren Kay Sims

est. 2015 | Boulder, Colorado

What was life like at the time you launched your influencer business? I started in October of 2015 while living in Dallas, Texas. I was 24 and had just recently gotten married. My husband was really supportive of me diving into this adventure 100% and believed in my potential as an influencer!

Did anyone help you start your influencer business? Yes! I actually started my career as a blogger with a friend of mine, Lauren Scruggs Kennedy. She already had an established blog that I followed, so I reached out to her and asked if she needed help. She was totally on board with that. I started my career as an influencer writing and working for her blog for about a year!

What inspired you to become an influencer? I'm passionate about encouraging and helping women to truly feel their absolute best, whether that's through putting together a killer outfit, finding a skincare routine that works for them, learning to rest and find balance, or getting in an awesome workout. I've always wanted to help women in those ways, and my blog allows me to do that.

How has having an influencer business changed your life? This business has 100% changed my life in ways I never could have dreamed. This job has allowed me to travel and see more of the world than I ever dreamed I would at 28 years old. My husband was able to quit his job and now helps me full time with the blog, and I love that this is an adventure we get to be on together. It truly has changed my life and made so many of my dreams come true in just a matter of a few years.

What has your experience as an influencer been like? Being an influencer has been the most incredible experience because the platform I have built has allowed me to connect with women and girls all over the world. My blog is all about promoting body positivity and helping women feel confident, no matter their shape or size. Having a voice to talk about these important topics is important to me and helping other curvy women feel represented in the fashion industry has been so fulfilling. We are all on our own self-love journey and I feel grateful that sharing mine has helped others feel more comfortable in their own skin.

Did you make any important decisions along the way that changed the trajectory of your business? I had been blogging for over two years and was seeing very little growth on my platform. I was working so hard and felt like it was not paying off. I soon realized that I wanted to do more than just be another person posting about pretty clothes—I wanted to do something that would help and inspire women. I wanted to make a difference in the world with my small corner of the internet. When I began opening up about my self-love journey and sharing my body-positive thoughts with my followers, that's when things began to change. Suddenly, I was connecting with so many women who were saying, "Finally a fashion blogger that looks like me!" or "I love your style and you're such a relatable size!" I made it my mission to show women that they don't have to be a size 2 to be chic.

What message do you want to inspire in your audience? All I've ever wanted readers to take away from *Sassy Red Lipstick* is this: You are beautiful just the way you are. I want to help you love yourself and I'd love to be your own personal cheerleader! No matter your shape or size, you can be confident, sexy, and successful. Believe it!

My blog is all about promoting body positivity and helping women feel confident no matter their shape or size.

❀ SASSYREDLIPSTICK

Sarah Tripp

est. 2013 | San Francisco, California

✪MOLLYBSIMS

Molly Sims

est. 2014 | Los Angeles, California

What were you doing before you launched your influencer business? I was hosting, acting, and modeling. I sort of did the whole influencer thing backwards.

Did anyone encourage you start your influencer business? I think my girlfriends were ultimately the ones who had me jumpstart my influencer business. I was always sharing information and products with them and then one day they were like, "You can do this as a living." And here we are.

What is the inspiration behind the content you create? My love for connecting people with products, tutorials, and makeovers. Whatever I used to tell my friends, I now tell everyone. I honestly get so much pleasure from sharing my favorites.

How has having an influencer business positively impacted your life? It has really helped me connect with my fans and my audience in terms of having a direct conversation, as opposed to just being photographed or interviewed. They truly get to see what my life is like.

Without all of my followers, I wouldn't be where I am today. I know people say that a lot, but it's true. I'm so lucky to be able to connect with all of them, and I truly appreciate all of the love and direct messages I receive on a daily basis. I read each and every message, and although I don't always have the time to respond, I'm very appreciative—they make my day!

❖ AWEDBYMONI

Monica O. Awe-Etuk

est. 2012 | Atlanta, Georgia

What was life like before you launched *Awed by Moni*? Before I started blogging full time, I had a very successful career in luxury retail for over 18 years. As a professional style consultant, my clients and friends would constantly say, "I wish I could take you home with me so you could style me every day." I solved that problem by creating my blog, and now I am able to go home with my followers, friends, and former clients every day.

What inspired you to launch *Awed by Moni*? While I was on maternity leave, my sister and I (we were both pregnant at the same time) decided we needed hobbies to ensure we had lives outside of our babies. She picked photography and I started a blog. I have to say I am happy she picked photography, because all of my top photos have been shot by her in Toronto. I picked blogging because of my love for fashion and people. I love how fashion and style make me feel and how it inspires my followers.

What advice would you give yourself if you could go back to when you were getting started with *Awed by Moni*? There is nothing I wish I could go back and tell myself. Every disappointment and every time I have accidentally deleted my website has made me more appreciative of the task of being an influencer. I truly believe I appreciate this platform more because success wasn't an easy road. I do not take my followers, collaborations, or success for granted.

As a professional style consultant, my clients and friends would constantly say, "I wish I could take you home with me so you could style me every day." I solved that problem by creating my blog…

liketoknow.it/**jessi_afshin**

⚙ JESSI_AFSHIN

Jessi Afshin

est. 2013 | Austin, Texas

What's the story behind your blog's name? How did you choose the name? I launched my blog at the age of 20, calling it *The Darling Detail.* "Darling" is our brand word—it's classic, timeless, chic, feminine; it never goes out of style. *The Darling Detail* is aimed at being an encouraging and inspiring platform. With the values of fashion + family + faith, we're working on transforming this space to be focused heavily on encouragement in every area of life: fashion, spirituality, wellness, beauty, and emotional and relational growth. The aim is not to paint a perfect or filtered life, but to bring out the vulnerability, transparency, and the messiness of life and encourage others through it all.

How has *The Darling Detail* changed your life? *The Darling Detail* has brought my family together. My first contracted resource was my talented brother who was principal photographer for the blog for over four years. The second was my mom, my marketing/product/financial manager, who truly made this business possible. And my father was incredibly generous in providing loans for my business at various turns. This business is about family—not just my immediate family—but my family of followers as well. I truly see my followers as my family.

What advice would you give your readers who want to follow in your footsteps? In a world managed by algorithms and a filtered reality, it's important to remember to be yourself because you're the most beautiful that way. Stay encouraged, and when you fail, don't only try again—but also learn from your mistakes. Be open to change, and be open to your business being shaped and molded as you grow with it. The result may not be what you planned or originally imagined, but don't be discouraged by that. Stay focused on a larger purpose—on helping those around you. That's where the ultimate joy and peace is found.

Do you have a favorite quote? "We won't be distracted by comparison if we're captivated with purpose." – Bob Goff

I spent a lot of my younger career watching where everyone else was going instead of driving in my own one-lane track. Kendra Scott says, "If you're doing what everyone is doing, you've already failed." In an over-saturated industry, your best asset is staying true to yourself.

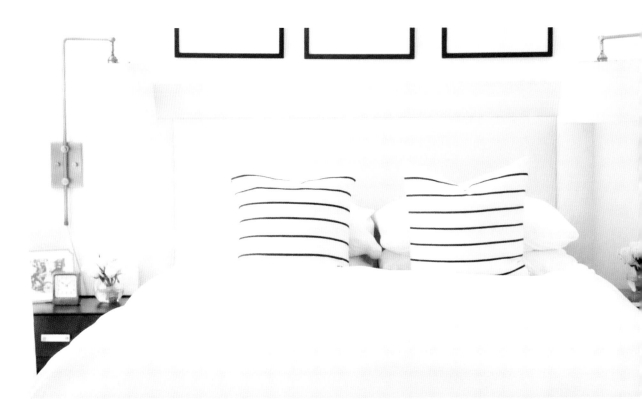

We wanted to hear from women like us who were trying to figure their lives out on a budget.

☉THEEVERYGIRL_

Alaina Kaczmarski and Danielle Moss

est. 2012 | Chicago, Illinois

What year did you start *The Everygirl*? We launched *The Everygirl* in 2012 when we were 26 and 28 years old living in Chicago and both blogging personally. We wanted to create a larger online media destination that was less like a blog and more like a magazine in terms of its content, staffing, and structure.

Did anyone help you start your influencer business? The two of us produced most of the content leading up to the launch—Danielle photographing, Alaina writing, styling, and doing graphics—but we quickly developed an amazing network of contributors that allowed us to grow and develop the brand. Writers, photographers, and stylists around the country wanted to contribute articles, home tours, and fashion pieces. Women wanted to share their talents and stories and believed in our mission. We had several women asking to intern with us in Chicago—they just wanted to be a part of it in any way. It was really

incredible. Now we have a team of nine full-time editors and a vast network of contributors around the world.

What was the inspiration behind *The Everygirl*? There was a void of relatable, attainable content in the online world, especially among lifestyle blogs. We wanted to hear from women like us who were trying to figure their lives out on a budget. From decorating their home and creating the perfect capsule wardrobe, to finding their dream job and traveling internationally, we wanted to inspire young women to live their best lives.

What do you wish you could go back and tell your yourself before you launched *The Everygirl*? Not everyone will like you. Or get you. Or believe in you. Or even want to see you succeed. And that's A-Okay. If you believe in yourself, love what you're doing, and have integrity in your work, that's all that matters.

⊗HALLIEDAILY

Hallie Swanson

est. 2010 | Los Angeles, California

What were you doing before you launched *HallieDaily*.com? When I still lived in China, I was a television sports reporter for a couple years, and then I worked as a Chinese foreign affairs officer, responsible for cultural and economic exchanges between Chinese government agencies and foreign countries around the world. I actually met my husband when I was leading one of those government tours to California, and things just clicked between us.

When did you launch your digital brand? It was 2010 when I started HallieDaily.com. I moved to Los Angeles in 2007 when I got married, and in 2008, our son, Red Bear, was born. I actually started my blog to document my new life in America to stay in touch with friends from China (that's why I publish in both English and Chinese), and to explore fashion.

Luckily for me, my husband has been an avid photographer practically his entire life, and even had his own photo studio when he was in college. Now I am lucky to have him as my own personal photographer and my business partner, too! He is the person who advised me to publish my blog in English and Chinese because he understands the growing importance of the Chinese market in the world. He showed me that it is an advantage that I am Chinese and can relate to both Western and Eastern cultures. It's a lot more challenging to publish in two languages—the internet platforms that are open in China are different than those open in the West, not to mention the time it takes to translate everything carefully. My husband advised me not to give up on the Chinese market just because it would be easier to do so. It's more work, but I'm glad I followed his recommendation! The love I get from my Chinese followers adds so much to the love I get from my U.S. and international followers; it's well worth the effort. I give deep thanks to all my dearest, darling readers and friends who are always there giving me support. I wish I could meet each of them in person, but I'm so thankful that I have gained so many relationships over the internet.

The business has not only helped me melt into the U.S. mainstream community as a new immigrant, but I am also happy to keep my business career ambitions going while I enjoy my stay-at-home wife and mom roles. It's a great combination for me! The internet made this business possible for me.

⊚THEFOXANDSHE

Blair Staky

est. 2012 | Chicago, Illinois

What inspired you to launch *The Fox and She*? I was running a full-time web design business that specialized in Wordpress blog designs for influencers and I became very immersed in that world. I was working with influencers on their sites all day, every day and I already loved to blog, so I figured, why not!

I started thinking of *The Fox and She* more as a business about two years after I launched it. I told my husband that I wanted to try and turn my blog into my full-time job so that when we had kids I would be able to work on my own schedule. He was really supportive and the following years were spent building and growing my blog. Today, I'm able to be home with our son and do the whole mom thing, but still have something for myself that makes me feel like I'm contributing more to our family, which is really important to me.

What advice would you give someone who is looking to start a career as an influencer? The influencer world is a big space and there's enough room for everyone to get a piece of the pie. When I first started, I thought I needed to fit a specific mold to be considered an influencer and I quickly learned that's not true. Being yourself is what makes you unique, so stay true to what you believe in and you'll be more successful than if you're trying to be someone else.

What is your favorite quote? Why does it resonate with you? "Buy the ticket, take the ride."

If you're passionate about something, go for it. Whether or not it works out, the journey and experience along the way will be worth it. I never want to look back and think, "Wow, I really wish I had just done or tried XYZ." I've had more failed business attempts than I care to mention, but each one taught me something and eventually led to *The Fox and She*, which finally stuck. You never know what you'll uncover about yourself along the way if you don't at least try!

⊛SHEAFFERTOLDMETO

Sheaffer Sims

est. 2012 | McKinney, Texas

When did you start *Sheaffer Told Me To*? Where were you living? I started my blog in 2012 while living in McKinney, Texas with my husband and son.

What were you doing before you launched *Sheaffer Told Me To*? When I started the blog, I was working part-time as a speech language pathologist for McKinney ISD, while also doing private therapy on the side. My focus was with children on the Autism spectrum, and I absolutely loved my job and the children, family, and other professionals I worked with at the time. Balancing work life, family life (I had a 4-year-old at the time), and the blog was too much to balance and something had to give. At that time, we made the decision for me to give full-time blogging a try.

How has having an influencer business impacted your life? Being a blogger is obviously quite different than being a speech language pathologist, but both arenas have allowed me to help people, and helping people brings me joy. The thing I loved most about my job as a speech therapist was the feedback I would get from the families about how their kids were becoming more functional in their everyday lives. When leaving my first job, I was very concerned that I was going to miss the human contact and the joy I got from helping others. I was not expecting that blogging would bring me similar joy, so it's been such an unexpected gift. Women have told me that they feel like they are better wives and mothers because they now feel good about themselves again, an emotion that they had somehow lost along the way of a busy life. My influence is different now, but I'm happy and thankful to still be making a positive impact in the lives of others.

My absolute favorite thing I do on my blog is host "Special Mama Giveaways." When working as a speech therapist, I developed a heart for all of the mamas I worked with that were giving *everything* they had to their precious kids. I saw that they were spending no money on themselves, and that a large majority of the family's money was going toward therapy sessions, doctor's appointments, special equipment, special diets, etc. for their child with special needs. Several times a year I host little giveaways to treat these mamas, and once a year I go all out and treat one of these very special mamas to a big shopping spree. I go shopping with them, take them to lunch, and hope they walk away feeling special and appreciated.

⊗ OHHCOUTURE

Leonie Hanne

est. 2014 | Hamburg, Germany

What inspired you to launch *Ohh Couture*? I've always loved fashion and worked part time in a boutique during high school and university. I really enjoyed styling and began to sell clothes online in the evenings on Germany's biggest re-commerce platform. I styled looks and took pictures with my roommate, and after a few weeks, we had tons of traffic on our profile and so many followers who were asking for more outfits and for us to start a blog or social media account. I finally decided to start my own blog and things moved really quickly.

What was your career before you launched your influencer business? I studied business administration, and afterwards, fashion management. Then I worked at Germany´s biggest online retailer as strategy consultant.

What advice would you give yourself if you could go back in time to when you first started *Ohh Couture*? Always trust your intuition and surround yourself with people who see you for who you are and not for what you could be for them.

What has been the most challenging thing about having an influencer business? Being self-employed means that you are completely responsible for your own business and success— something which is super inspiring, but also results in sleepless nights because there is always something you could be doing to improve your business.

"

I realized this could be not only mentally and spiritually fulfilling, but also financially enriching.

⊙ SIMPLYCYN

Cynthia Andrew

est. 2010 | Queens, New York

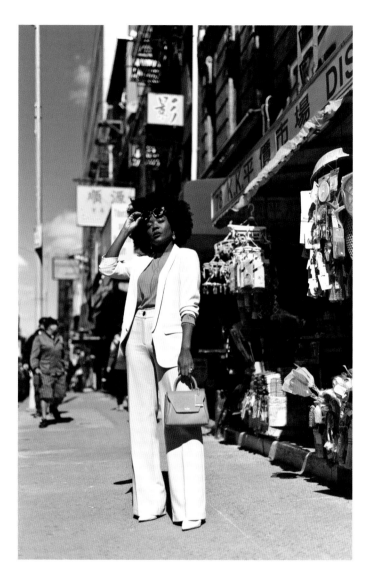

What were you doing before you launched your influencer business? I'm still doing it! I'm an attorney, and over the past couple of years, have transitioned from trusts and estates litigation to regulatory compliance. My influencer business is my second gig.

What inspired you to launch *SimplyCyn*? I was inspired to start it as a hobby because I needed an outlet for my creative spirit. I have been able to treat it as a business as so many other influencers out there

have, and because amazing opportunities presented themselves. I realized this could be not only mentally and spiritually fulfilling, but also financially enriching.

What has been the most challenging thing about running *SimplyCyn*? Managing a variety of projects and handling the demands on the social media front. It's kind of a non-stop gig. You have to know when to go and when to slow down.

❂LOUISEROE

Louise Roe

est. 2015 | Los Angeles, California

What were you doing before you launched your influencer business? I was hosting a makeover show on MTV called *Plain Jane,* and was the Fashion Editor-at-Large for *Glamour* Magazine.

How did you come up with the name for your blog, *Front Roe*? I'd used the title for a magazine column I'd written in the UK, and then for my book. I wrote a style guide to answer lots of the questions I was getting on social media. Halfway through writing it, I figured I really needed an online version of the book that would be full of ideas and advice, so *Front Roe by Louise Roe* was born! The name just came out one day—it's a play on my last name and the idea of not just sitting front row at fashion week, but sitting front row in your own life. Instilling confidence in the women I've made over on shows or the women I chat with through my blog and social media is honestly the core of what I do and why I do it. It makes me happy!

What inspired you to launch your influencer business? Prior to working in TV, I had worked in magazines. I was the News Editor at Vogue.com in London, writing all the stories and coding when it was all pretty basic! Most magazines didn't even have a website yet, which shows how long ago this was. Cut to a few years later living in Los Angeles, and I really began to miss styling shoots and writing articles. I have always loved writing more than anything—my dad is a writer—and I love that escapism. So, I launched the blog to create my own version of a magazine and to talk more closely and regularly with my followers. The community grew quickly, but very organically, and turning it into a business was secondary. I went in with the goal of creating interesting, beautiful content, and making money from it came along a few months later. I still think that's an important way to approach any business, if you can. Strike up the passion and integrity first, and the financial rewards will come.

✸RANDIGARRETTDESIGN

Randi Garrett

est. 2016 | Phoenix, Arizona

When and where did *Randi Garrett Design* get its start? I started *Randi Garrett Design* in 2016 when I was 39 years old and living in a small town in Arizona.

Is *Randi Garrett Design* your full-time job? I am a full-time wife, mother (and recent puppy mama) first, but *Randi Garrett Design* is my second full-time job! I spend many hours in the laundry room, at the kitchen counter doing homework and pushing two completely full grocery carts through the grocery store. I fall asleep with my laptop in my lap scrolling through photos, I buy ridiculous amounts of fresh flowers, and have over 12,000 photos on my phone. Some call me Super Woman. I say, "No, silly, I am just Super *Crazy*!"

The best part about my influencer business is that I can be as busy or as free as I would like to be. If my kids need me one day, I don't plan collaborations around that day. If I am stressed out, I post less often and take a break. Being a wife and mom comes first. Sharing my tips for living life in style comes second. If my life is less than stylish at the moment, I focus on taking care of things on the home front. *Randi Garrett Design* is my passion, but my family is my heart and soul.

How has *Randi Garrett Design* changed your life? *Randi Garrett Design* has changed my life in ways I never thought possible. Most importantly, I have made friendships that will last a lifetime. I have met a circle of women who love and support each other. Who cheer each other on. I have been able to help friends and followers make their homes more inspiring places to be. There is nothing better than receiving emails and messages from readers who have made their homes a little better through my inspiration.

What is your favorite quote? How does it resonate with you? "Be kind to everyone you meet, for everyone is fighting a hard battle."

No one's life is perfect, no matter how perfect it may seem from the outside. Everyone needs kindness. If you ever have a thought to do something or say something nice to someone, act on it. You will never be sorry. If someone is mean or unkind, it is probably because they have something amiss in their life. Instead of snapping back, pay them a compliment, do something nice. Our world would be a better place if we treated everyone this way.

⊘DTHOMPSY

Destiny Thompson

est. 2015 | Salt Lake City, Utah

When did you start your blog, *Truly Destiny*, and how did you come up with the name? I started my blog, *Truly Destiny,* in 2015. I was 23 years old, just had my first child, Truman, and made a move to Houston, Texas. My blog is named after my son, Truman. His nickname is Tru, so I used Truly as a play off his name. I thought it was the perfect name because I only share things I truly love and am passionate about.

Did anyone help you start your influencer business? My husband took all of my photos. We worked together to get my business started. I remember working on my blog late at night for a month straight after putting my son to bed. I couldn't afford a fancy website at first, so I did tons of research and got it up and running all on my own!

How has having an influencer business changed your life? Having my influencer business has definitely blessed my family's life in so many ways. There is nothing more satisfying than being a working mom with a degree that took hard work and sacrifice, while still having the ability and the time to give your children all the nurture and love they need.

What do you wish you could go back and tell yourself? I wish I would have started sooner and would have been more confident. It's always scary putting yourself out there, but I am so happy I did! Own who you are and what makes you special and unique.

One thing to keep in mind is that our photos portray our best life, not our real life. Glamorous things aside, there are a lot of heartaches and tears poured into the business that people don't often see.

◉NOTJESSFASHION

Jessica Wang

est. 2014 | New York City, New York

funny enough, it happened by accident.

What were you doing before you launched your influencer business? I majored in finance during college and was recruited by Morgan Stanley during my senior year. Immediately after I graduated, I made my way to the Big Apple.

What inspired you to launch *Not Jess Fashion*? Funny enough, it happened by accident. I had this idea of starting an online boutique. I thought that starting a blog would be a good way to drive some traffic to the store. To my surprise, more people took interest in my style and content than I expected, so I decided to stay the course and haven't looked back since.

I realized early on that I could provide a space where people could escape and my blog became that medium. My style and photography have evolved over the years, but the voice remains the same. My blog covers everything from fashion, beauty, travel, family, and food. It's now evolved to even include blogging tips!

What is the biggest misconception about influencers? One thing to keep in mind is that our photos portray our best life, not our real life. Glamorous things aside, there are a lot of heartaches and tears poured into the business that people don't often see.

I remind myself every day that it is so important to run your own race. At the end of the day, it's beautiful imagery, not real life.

⊛ LONESTARSOUTHERN

Kate Padgitt

est. 2013 | Dallas, Texas

Is your influencer business your full-time job? By the time I reached my senior year of college, I had been blogging for about a year and a half and had seen that with hard work, it was possible to earn money from what I was doing. In my heart, I wanted to blog full time but wasn't sure if making the leap was a wise decision. I knew I wouldn't be able to work a full-time job and blog on the side—I just poured too much into it that it would leave little time for anything else in my life. So I came to a "blog full time or quit" moment.

When my parents, who are very practically minded and always raised me with that perspective, told me they thought it was a good idea to try blogging full time, my mind was made up. I moved in with my parents to "try it out" for a year, and realized my dreams of becoming a full-time blogger were turning into a reality. The spring after graduating, I was able to move out and haven't looked back!

What is your favorite quote? "Don't compare your beginning to someone else's middle."

I remember coming across this early on in blogging and it felt like a breath of fresh air to repeat in my head. It's so easy to compare yourself to others much further down the blogging path and feel like you're not doing enough. I remind myself every day that it's so important to remember to run your own race. At the end of the day, it's beautiful imagery, not real life. So, as cliché as it is to say, I think it's so important to continue to emphasize the importance of not comparing yourself to what you see on social media, especially when what you're comparing yourself to is someone's full-time job. Yes, the photo may be gorgeous, but the hours of staging and editing that went into the back end were definitely not as glamorous.

What were you doing before you became an influencer? I was in college in Ireland studying business. Then, as soon as I finished, I moved to New York City to work full time as a social media manager for a designer before going full time with *Retro Flame* in 2016.

What inspired you to launch *Retro Flame*? I know it's a little cringey and everyone probably says the same thing, but it really did come from passion. I truly believe that the best way to start a business is to not even realize you're starting one. When it's truly your passion, it will never feel like work. I grew up in a really small village in Ireland and when I started my blog, it felt like I was finally able to connect with a community I was so excited to be part of. It was a feeling I had never experienced before and I just got hooked! I put every ounce of my energy into it and the ability to keep improving always inspired me to keep going. I definitely was a little on the shy side growing up, and without even realizing it at the time, having a blog gave me so much confidence.

Who has been the biggest supporter of your career as an influencer? I more or less launched *Retro Flame* all by myself, but honestly, I probably would have quit a long time ago if not for the support of my family. They really didn't know what I was doing taking endless outfit photos in our back garden in Ireland, but they supported me 110% every step of the way. My mom and sister took all of my early photos and then after a year or two, I started to work with some photographers.

About four years after I started, my sister, Kaelin, joined the team and now I genuinely can't even remember *Retro Flame* without her! It's been so fun having her work with me every day and she has definitely brought a new side to the brand.

✪ RETROFLAME

Erika Fox

est. 2012 | New York City, New York

❂JOHNPHILP3

John Philp Thompson III

est. 2016 | Chicago, Illinois

What were you doing before you launched your influencer business? I attended the University of Texas at Austin where I studied political science. My first job out of college was with a boutique PR and communications agency that specialized in the nutrition space.

What inspired you to begin creating content as an influencer? I was friends with quite a few fashion and menswear bloggers and took many of their photos. Two of my favorite (and Chicago's only!) menswear shops closed that year, so I felt like I had no outlet for menswear in the Midwest and had to attempt to give it a voice!

Is your influencer business your full-time job? Yes! I've been fortunate enough to be working for myself since 2014. Because I was already freelancing as a photographer, I slowly transitioned to more of a blogger role with my blog, riskyjackal.com.

How has your influencer business positively impacted your life? It's allowed me to travel and see so much of the world, which I'm so grateful for. I've met so many amazing people on this journey and have been able to work with brands that I love and respect.

What inspired you to launch your influencer business? I come from a family of entrepreneurs, so the idea of starting a business was not farfetched. Although I felt blessed to have been able to stay at home with my children, the monotony pushed me to find something that would exercise the creative muscles I had neglected while away from my career in retail management. Thank goodness for muscle memory! Merging my affinity for fashion and style with my experiences as a woman, wife, and mother came naturally to me once I began.

How did you come up with the name *Newtexacali*? I chose the name because I live in Texas, my sister lived in New York, and one of my closest friends lives in California. They are both entrepreneurs who I look up to, so I merged the names of the three states and *NewTexaCali* was born!

How has having an influencer business changed your life? Creating an influencer business has changed my life by letting me know that when you're doing something you love, it doesn't feel like "work." In just a short time, I created a business that not only helps support my family, but also provides me with the opportunity to be home with them. I also take pride in the idea that I can be an inspiration to all women by being able to speak my truth through my blog. Receiving messages and having conversations with women I've never met through shared experiences has been life changing—I love it!

Is there anyone along the way who helped you grow your business? My photographer, Bri Costello! We had a chance meeting at a restaurant almost two years ago. We lost contact for a while, but a year later, she emailed me and said she'd love to work together. The rest is history. I don't think I'd be as successful without her!

Creating an influencer business has changed my life by letting me know that when you're doing something you love, it doesn't feel like "work."

❂ NEWTEXACALI

Nikki Gamble

est. 2016 | Houston, Texas

⊚ COULDIHAVETHAT

Samantha Wennerstrom

est. 2009 | Santa Barbara, California

What year did you start *Could I Have That?* I started my blog, *Could I Have That?*, in 2009 as a creative outlet. I was 26 years old and working at a small city magazine as an editorial assistant in Santa Barbara. It was during the recession and budgets were getting cut left and right. I wanted to write more, so I started a blog to house all the things I wanted to write about, share, and photograph.

How did you come up with the name, *Could I Have That?* It was a joke between me and my sister when we shopped or wanted something badly.

How has having an influencer business changed your life? I've been able to travel to places I never thought I would go, meet some seriously inspiring successful people, and most of all, it's given me a sense of confidence I didn't have before.

What do you wish you could go back and tell your nascent influencer self? Get some sleep! I would stay up past midnight sometimes working.

Where are you living now? I still live in Santa Barbara with my husband and 3-year-old daughter.

◉ CMCOVING

Caitlin Covington

Est. 2011 | Winston Salem, North Carolina

How did your digital brand get its start? I started my blog in 2011 when I was a junior in college at the University of North Carolina at Chapel Hill. I started my blog, *Southern Curls and Pearls*, as a hobby. I wanted to work for a magazine after graduation and I thought of my blog as a resume to show potential employers my writing abilities. I wrote about my life in college and my sorority, as well as healthy recipes and fashion, but as I gained readers, I realized that they mainly wanted to see fashion posts, so that's where I focused my efforts.

Has anyone been influential to the success of your business? My mom has been an influential part of my business from the very beginning! She captured my photos for many years for free. We taught ourselves everything—from taking photos in manual and what

camera and equipment to use, to photo editing. I was eventually able to hire her as a paid employee when my blog became profitable and she still takes my photos to this day. I love getting to travel the world with her!

How has having your digital brand changed your life? Honestly, this industry has changed my entire life! If I had never started a blog, I would still be the same person that I am today, but blogging has given me the ability to work from home and be my own boss. It is sometimes difficult to have a work-life balance— it's tempting to work 24/7, since we all know that the social media world never sleeps! Despite the 80-hour work weeks, there are some amazing perks to being an influencer—one of them is getting to travel the world with my mom and husband, and for that, I am truly thankful.

How did you choose the name of your blog? What inspired you to start? The blog is associated with my e-commerce hijab brand, Haute Hijab. I chose the name because "haute" in French means 'high' or 'elevated.' In essence, my aim was to elevate hijab. I started *Haute Hijab* to provide Muslim women with access to high-quality, beautiful hijabs, and to empower them to feel confident in their identity as Muslim women.

How has having your influencer business changed your life? My business got so big that I eventually quit my job as an attorney to focus on *Haute Hijab* full time. It also led to my move to NYC, which was absolutely life-changing. It's still my favorite city in the world (having lived abroad for 4 years, we've traveled to some pretty sweet places) and I can't believe I actually live here. It's such a dream!

What is your favorite quote? What does it mean to you? "Don't try to be something for everyone, just be everything to someone."

I know exactly who my audience is and I'm okay with alienating those who don't understand me as an American Muslim. There's not much I can do about that. But what is in my control is the positive influence I can have on Muslim women—so I run with it.

Don't try to be something for everyone, just be everything to someone.

❋HAUTEHIJAB

Melanie Elturk

est. 2010 | New York City, New York

✪ ZDESIGNATHOME

Zabrina Hancock

est. 2016 | Houston, Texas

When did you launch your blog, *ZDesign at Home*? I started *ZDesign at Home* in 2016 while living in Midland, Texas at the age of 46. Before that, I was designing and decorating for clients, and being a stay-at-home mom!

Did anyone encourage you to get started? Yes! I work with a great group of women I met through social media and blogging. We bounce ideas off of one another and support each other in order to help each individual in the group succeed in this wonderful world of influence.

Is there anything you wish you could go back and tell yourself before you launched your blog? I would prepare myself for the hard work it takes to get this business off the ground—it's important to keep the momentum going but also important to get help when you need it.

#LTKfamily

These influencers make motherhood a little easier for everyone. From bump style to life with little ones, they share shopping tips and life lessons fit for the whole family.

⦿ *simplyxclassic*
Miriam Gin
est. 2012 | Orange County, California

⦿ *thefashionbugblog*
Laura Wills
est. 2014 | London, United Kingdom

est. 2013 | Rogers, Arkansas
Tara Gibson
⊕ *themrsgibby*

est. 2015 | Houston, Texas
Kate Blue
⊕ *kateireneblue*

Follow @liketoknow.it.family and find
everything from #LTKbump-friendly styles
to #LTKbaby and #LTKkids picks in the
LIKEtoKNOW.it app.

⊕ *shaymone*
Shay Sweeney
est. 2016 | Houston, Texas

THEMOMEDIT

Shana Draugelis

est. 2008 | Philadelphia, Pennsylvania

When did you launch your blog, *The Mom Edit*? Did anyone help you get started? I started my blog in 2008 after the birth of my first son. Blogging was a hobby; a creative outlet. In those days I was struggling with how to redefine myself in this new context of "mother." The writing was a way for me to process these changes and writing about the tough stuff helped me feel more connected, like I wasn't alone.

My husband has always been my biggest fan. He understood (better than I did) that blogging—the writing, the connection with readers—helped me stay fulfilled. Now he helps with the analytics and advertising and our business is truly a team effort.

What was life like before you started your career as an influencer? When my oldest was born, I had been working as an engineer at Lockheed Martin for the past 10 years. I was the chief lab architect for SBIRS Ground, a space-based missile-warning system. It was a demanding and addicting job—I *loved* it. The out-of-the-box thinking required to solve complex problems as an engineer is a skill set that can be applied anywhere.

How has your brand evolved since it launched in 2008? Ahh…the first name of my blog was *Ain't No Mom Jeans*, but I changed the name because, thankfully, the dowdy mom stereotype had all but vanished! Mom jeans were suddenly cool again and thanks to the influx of mom bloggers, the word "mom" was no longer a bad word.

I chose the name *The Mom Edit* because I wanted to merge the practicality that #momlife requires with current trends or styles. I truly believe that moms can, and should, wear whatever the heck they want…it's just that most of us need a slightly more practical version than we did before. It's like real life…with a slight mom edit.

The Mom Edit now has team members all over the US, and I'm really proud that we're enabling women to work the hours they want, to be creative, and still help support their families.

Was there anything along the way that changed the trajectory of your business? In May of 2013, I was diagnosed with breast cancer. Initially, I thought about shutting down the blog—certainly, my readers would understand! But what I ultimately learned by sharing my battle with breast cancer was that this blog was not only a fledgling business, but more importantly, a community. My relationship with my readers strengthened, and instead of walking away from blogging, I became more determined than ever to honor that community. I feel very lucky to have the readers I have—their comments over the years have been wise, supportive, challenging, and insightful—and whether they realize it or not, they have played a major role in shaping the direction of *The Mom Edit*. We're a much more playful and helpful space because of our readers.

◉ STYLEDSNAPSHOTS

Kendall Kremer

est. 2013 | New York City, New York

When did you start *Styled Snapshots*? How old were you? Where were you living? At the age of 25, living in New York City, on September 13, 2013, I decided to hit "publish" on my very first blog post on StyledSnapshots.com—a day I will never forget. I had no idea what I was doing, the journey that lay before me, and the incredible people I would meet along the way. Who knew this tiny piece of the internet that I owned would one day define me as a businesswoman and influencer to many.

Did anyone support you along the way? In the very beginning, I was doing everything by myself. I would trek up onto our unfinished roof of our apartment building, set up my tripod, and start snapping away. At the time, I was too embarrassed to take photos on the streets, so this was my solution. Fast forward a few months and through a lot of trial and error,

my boyfriend (now husband) started getting behind the camera and helping me make my vision a reality. He has been my rock, #1 fan, and biggest supporter through this crazy ride.

Did you have another career before you launched *Styled Snapshots*? Before I launched my business as an influencer, I was working full time as a child life specialist on the day surgery unit at a hospital in New York City. This was my passion and what I went to school for, so I made both work for as long as I could. As the years passed by and my blog grew, I realized I couldn't give my all to both careers. Finally, when it officially became too much to juggle, I felt peace in closing one chapter of my life to continue the next. While scary at first, I honestly I have no regrets and have never felt so empowered as a woman!

What were you doing before you launched *Frank Vinyl*? I was studying graphic design and interning for graphic design firms. After that, I was waitressing, doing some wedding photography, and also fashion styling to keep the money coming in until I figured things out.

How did you come up with the name *Frank Vinyl*? I wanted to use my name so I could always branch out into other categories if I wanted to. Music has always been a big inspiration for me. I am a big lover of vinyl and old school bands like The Beatles, The Doors, and Jimi Hendrix. I liked vinyl because music is what always inspires me.

What has been your biggest realization as an influencer? Who or what has helped you realize this? I think realizing that I couldn't do it all on my own was a big step forward for me. I realized that giving up a bit of control would actually help me in the long run. I now have people that help me with different areas of my business including my go-to photographers, someone to help me strategize, web designers, a manager, and blogger friends for support.

What is your favorite quote? What does it mean to you? "We are all perfect in our imperfections."

I have always loved this quote because it reminds me that every person has something unique to only them that no one else can replicate. I find that anything that is "too" perfect can be boring. Imperfection is always more interesting!

Every person has something unique to only them that no one else can replicate.

❂ FRANKVINYL

Francesca Felix Smith

est. 2010 | San Diego, California

◉JESSANNKIRBY

Jess Ann Kirby

est. 2013 | Newport, Rhode Island

Where were you working before you launched your blog? What inspired you to launch it? I worked as a project manager at an HR consulting firm. I was really unhappy at my job and wanted to do something different. I wanted to work in fashion, so I figured starting a blog would help open the door for an opportunity in the industry.

How has being an influencer changed your life? It's pretty amazing that my boyfriend, Craig, and I run this business together and have accomplished things we never dreamed of five years ago. I never thought I'd be a person that owned my own business and worked for myself. Now I can't imagine doing anything else. It's a 24/7 job, but it is also incredibly rewarding. We bought our first house this past year and we travel often. This job has its challenges, but it also has given me a lot of freedom.

What is your favorite quote? What does it mean to you? Before my aunt passed away, she said, "You have to find what you love and do that." She was the main reason I started my blog.

What do you wish you could go back and tell yourself before launching your influencer business? I wish I connected more with my readers and followers early on. I've always been a very private person and an introvert so it was a challenge for me to share personal details in the beginning. It took me a few years to really open up, but it was a very rewarding experience and ultimately created and fostered an incredible community.

⊗ PALEOMG

Juli Bauer Roth

est. 2011 | Denver, Colorado

What inspired you to launch *PaleOMG*? I decided to start *PaleOMG* because I felt so lost when I first decided to change the way I ate and I didn't want others to feel that way. I wanted people to feel confident when it came to eating healthier and taking care of themselves. I wanted to prove to people that they could eat delicious food all while making better choices in their diet. I think people often feel more confident in their decisions when they see their peers take the first step. I wanted my blog to be that first step for many.

How has having an influencer business changed your life? Before *PaleOMG* became my full-time job, I was living paycheck to paycheck, barely able to pay rent some months. But once *PaleOMG* became my full-time job, it gave me so much freedom. Not only was I able to pay off any debt I had, purchase our first home, and begin to create a retirement plan for the future, but I was able to find a business that kept me motivated, excited, and working hard day after day.

I've created over 800 recipes, written three cookbooks, started my own podcast, partnered with an amazing company to create my own activewear line, and I've been lucky enough to work with fantastic brands that have changed my life for the better. Every day I'm able to create a wonderful life for me and my family, but I'm also helping others create a better life for themselves, too. It's pretty amazing.

What is one of your favorite quotes? "Failing to plan is planning to fail."

I strongly believe that a business like this takes constant planning. If you're not planning, you're already behind—it's what keeps me motivated and excited for what's to come in the future!

> I think people often feel more confident in their decisions when they see their peers take the first step. I wanted my blog to be that first step for many.

What were you doing before you launched your influencer business? I had just finished my degree in fashion design and communication. The summer before graduating, I had completed two internships in New York working within the fashion industry at magazines and an online site. When I graduated, I started traveling all through Europe but eventually ran out of money and had to come home to work a few jobs. I started working at a small boutique in my hometown, where I had a lot of creative freedom to play around with visual merchandising and social output. I admired the owner and her entrepreneurial qualities—she was always pushing me to do more and it really helped me with wanting to start my own brand. I loved social media but I felt I had so much more to share and discuss. I also knew I was moving to Berlin, so naturally I wanted to start the blog to share my new experiences with friends and family.

How did you choose the name _Not Your Standard_ for your blog? I always wanted to share a standard of living, so I was stuck on the word "standard" for quite some time. Eventually, I was talking to someone and I kept saying, "I don't want it to be a standard fashion blog, I want it to be so much more," and somehow, the words _Not Your Standard_ were born.

What has been the most challenging thing about being an influencer? The constant doubt. You have so many highs in this business and then so many lows. It can be easy to compare yourself to everyone else in the influencer world. I find that during those times, it's best to take a step back and just reevaluate where you want to go with your brand. Ask yourself the tough questions and talk to someone you respect to have them offer critiques from an outsider's point of view. They can give you direction that you can't always get on your own.

What do you wish you could go back and tell yourself? To not be so scared about making mistakes, especially if you really feel it is right in your gut. Trusting my instinct has never failed me because even if it didn't work out, going that route allowed me to have clarity and guide me in the right direction.

❀NOTYOURSTANDARD

Kayla Seah

est. 2012 | Toronto, Ontario

My mind continues to be blown and I am eternally grateful to the girls who take the time out of their day to connect with me. Truly such an incredible gift.

✦KATHLEEN_BARNES

Kathleen Barnes

est. 2011 | San Francisco, California

When did you decide to become an influencer? I started my site, *Carrie Bradshaw Lied*, at the beginning of 2011 when I was moving from Birmingham, Alabama to Jackson, Mississippi. I was less than a year out of college and trying to keep my love of journalism alive because I couldn't get a job in publishing (thank you, economy of 2010).

Has having an influencer business changed your life? Oh my gosh, 100x over. My husband is finishing his medical training so it has supported our lives since I took *Carrie Bradshaw Lied* full time in 2015. We have taken photography classes, invested in professional equipment, joined a talent agency—I never thought I would be blogging full time when I started this "side hustle." My mind continues to be blown, and I am eternally grateful to the girls who take the time out of their day to connect with me. It is truly such an incredible gift.

What's your biggest challenge as an influencer? It's nonstop; 24/7. I work more now than I ever did at any of my corporate gigs.

What is your favorite quote? What does it mean to you? "Use what talents you possess; the woods would be very silent if no birds sang there except those that sang best." - Henry Van Dyke

I love this quote because it reminds me to stay in my lane, focus on being my best self, be original, and curate unique content that brings value to my readers.

Is *Style Charade* your full-time job? For the past 15+ years, I've worked full time in the public relations industry, and I continue to work at the same PR agency from when I first launched *Style Charade* in 2015 with my husband. I'm a big believer that you can be both a successful blogger and full-time professional.

How did you come up with the name *Style Charade*? Coming from a public relations background, branding has always been important to me. After brainstorming for a few months, the word "charade" kept coming to my mind. I loved the playfulness of the verb, especially knowing I wanted to create colorful, whimsical content.

Furthermore, one of my favorite movies of all time is Audrey Hepburn and Cary Grant's *Charade*. My brand has never been, nor will it ever be, designed to be an open book or accurate reflection of my life. I may be wearing a ball gown for no reason one day, and twirling in a pleated skirt the next. My photos are meant to be light-hearted, thumb-stopping images that make people smile.

Did anyone help you start *Style Charade*? My husband is the co-founder and has been my business partner since day one. Previously, I ran a bridal blog from 2008-2010, which gave me the opportunity to learn more about the blogosphere firsthand.

Do you have a favorite quote? "For beautiful eyes, look for the good in others; for beautiful lips, speak only words of kindness; and for poise, walk with the knowledge that you are never alone." - Audrey Hepburn

My photos are meant to be light-hearted, thumb-stopping images that make people smile.

⊚JENNIFERLAKE

Jennifer Lake

est. 2014 | Chicago, Illinois

⊚BECKIOWENS

Becki Owens

est. 2014 | San Clemente, California

What were you doing before you launched your influencer business? I was remodeling and building homes in the beach town where I am from. I'm a mother of four children, so my priority is spending time with them. Growing my social media presence was a great way for me to share my work and grow my business without having to compromise my role as mother. Balancing a growing design and influencer business while raising four kids adds up to more than full time. But l love it. There really never is a dull moment.

What inspired you to share your work on social media? I wanted to grow my interior design business and generate a platform where I could share my work and the beautiful inspiration from other interior designers. I love the creative community that comes with sharing through social media. It's been such an incredible tool to grow my design business and learn what people truly love and dream of in their own homes.

How has having an influencer business changed your life? It's created opportunities to work with wonderful clients from all over on amazing projects. It's also provided a great way to work from home and be a present, mindful parent, which is really important to me.

What do you wish you could go back and tell yourself when you started? Be confident and not afraid to put yourself out there. People will love you for who you are!

GIRLWITHCURVES

Tanesha Awasthi

est. 2011 | San Francisco, California

What year did you start your blog, *Girl With Curves*? How old were you? Where were you living? I started *Girl With Curves* on February 13, 2011, with no intention of it becoming the business it is today. At the time, I was a newlywed, freshly 30, going through a major professional rut in the midst of a big career promotion. Born and raised in Silicon Valley, I ended up in the tech field and was very good at what I was doing as an account manager at a network security company, but I felt a major lack of passion for my job. I longed to work in fashion, but I didn't know how since I was living in the San Francisco Bay Area and hadn't done any internships or anything remotely related to fashion.

After a few months of listening to me complain about all the regrets I had not pursuing a career in fashion, my husband (who's now my full-time business partner and photographer), suggested I start a style blog as a creative outlet. At the time, I had no idea what a style blogger was, if I'm being completely honest! And when he showed me a few style blogs online, I refused to pose for pictures—I thought it was ridiculous! I had tried modeling and hated it because I was never big on posing for pictures. After a couple weeks of him trying to convince me, I gave in and let him take photos of me in skinny jeans, over the knee boots, and a sweater at the park next to where we lived. He put the pictures up on Flickr and set a Google alert for my name. I didn't think anything would come out of it, but two weeks later I got an email that linked out to my images—

someone had posted on tumblr and gotten 400+ comments and likes, all of which were positive, referring to me being a "curvy girl." That very moment, I turned to my husband and said, "Okay, I'm going to start this blog and call it *Girl With Curves*."

How has having an influencer business changed your life? My husband and I run the business full time, and it's amazing how it's grown over the years from being my hobby to my full-time job, to now supporting our family. We love having the freedom to work from anywhere in the world, and work as much or as little as we'd like.

Was there anyone or anything along the way that changed the trajectory of your business? My former boss and CFO at my tech job, who's now a great friend, was the one who encouraged me to pursue the blog full time. Without his encouragement I wouldn't have, because I was so afraid of the unknown.

What is your favorite quote? What does it mean to you? "A woman's dress should be tight enough to show she's a woman and loose enough to show she's a lady."

This quote explains my personal style to a T! While I love and embrace my curvy shape, I don't find it necessary to show it all off, I'm kind of modest when it comes to the way I dress and what I choose to show the world.

✷KELLYINTHECITY

Kelly Larkin

est. 2013 | Chicago, Illinois

What were you doing before you launched your digital brand, *Kelly in the City*? I was a full-time 8th grade English teacher in South Bronx through the New York City Teaching Fellows, a fellowship program that places new teachers in hard-to-staff schools in the city. While I loved my job, I missed writing and photography—before I became a teacher, I briefly worked as a newspaper reporter, magazine editor, and wedding photographer. I also secretly pined to be involved in the New York City fashion scene. Blogging allowed me to teach, but also explore my other interests in my free time!

Did anyone help you launch *Kelly in the City*? My now-husband, Mitch, was instrumental in this. He and I worked together, so we jumped off the subway every day on our way home and he took my outfit photos. He also enlisted a few of his friends (who happened to be developers) to help me create the actual website. I'm beyond grateful for Mitch's support. Over the years, we've had more late nights than I could ever count and he has sacrificed so much in order to get the site to where it is today. Truthfully, *Kelly in the City* is half him; he's behind the scenes of every single post in some capacity. From the beginning of "us," our goal has been to one day own our own business and work side

by side. And many, many years later, we've finally reached that goal. We clock long hours and make a lot of sacrifices, but this is the life we've always wanted and we're incredibly proud of it.

Where do you live today? Mitch and I live in Chicago with our two-year-old daughter, Emma, and a four-year-old miniature dachshund, Noodle, who Emma has renamed "Beale." We don't know what to do. Should we change her name?!

What is one of your favorite quotes? What does it mean to you? "The best portion of a good man's life are his little, nameless, unremembered acts of kindness and love." -William Wordsworth.

This has been my favorite quote since high school when I discovered it in an English class. It's easy to get caught up in the unimportant things; the chaos and trivial parts of everyday life. But I think of this quote often. It reminds me that my life's purpose is to offer kindness and love to others and to build them up and help them realize just how amazing they are.

> Practice patience and do not take any of the road blocks (there will be many) so personally. Instead, use those "failures" as the drive you need to push forward.

⊛RANTIINREVIEW

Ranti Onayemi

est. 2013 | Denver, Colorado

What inspired you to launch your influencer business? As a child growing up in Lagos, Nigeria, I was in awe of my aunt, Juliet. She embodied what I wanted to be when I grew up. Stylish and accomplished, I remembered spending many hours right at her hip, watching everything she did. She was the first person to let me know my quirky sense of style, even as a child, was okay. I idolized her. She ran, and still runs, a successful fashion house which included a factory located in the compound of the house where I grew up. Consisting of about five tailors and a couple designers who helped bring her and her clients' vision to life, was a fascinating process to witness; I knew then I wanted to be in the fashion world when I grew up, just like her. Years later, I moved to the States and I did not see what I love in fashion depicted on the bodies of any of the ladies around me. Out of frustration and a way to channel all these ideas I had in my head, *Ranti In Review* began.

Did anyone help you launch your career as an influencer? My then-boyfriend, now-husband was very instrumental in helping start my blog. He is my photographer (despite also having a very demanding career as an architect), and he is my biggest support system.

Is *Ranti in Review* your full-time job? If not, what else do you do? I'm proud to say I wear quite a few hats. My influencer business makes up about 65% of what I do. I am also a personal stylist, luxury goods consigner, and interior designer to support the diverse needs of many of my clients.

Is there anything you wish you could go back and tell yourself before you launched your influencer business? If I could go back and tell my past influencer self anything, it would be to practice patience and do not take any of the road blocks (there will be many) so personally. Instead, use those "failures" as the drive you need to push forward.

⊙JYO_SHANKAR

Jyo Shankar

est. 2013 | San Francisco, California

When did you start your influencer business? How old were you? Where were you living? I started my blog, *Jyo Shankar*, in 2013. I was 29 years old and living in the San Francisco Bay Area.

Did anyone help you kick off your career as an influencer? My husband, who is also my photographer, web designer, and blog manager. Being an influencer has given us the opportunity to work together on something we both love! He has a full-time job aside from this, but his free time is dedicated to helping me with the blog.

What has been your biggest challenge as an influencer? As an influencer, you have to wear so many different hats. You have to be the model, editor, web designer, marketing professional, etc. all at once.

☒THESPOILEDHOME

Sandi Johnson and Shalia Ashcraft

est. 2015 | Dale, Oklahoma and Seminole, Oklahoma

How did you meet? How did you decide to start an influencer business together? We began our business in January of 2015 and we had no clue what we were doing. Sandi was 35 at the time and I was 48. We were both living in Seminole, Oklahoma. Before we started, Sandi was a hairstylist and I was a high school English teacher—we met when Sandi started doing my hair.

How did you come up with the name of your digital brand, *The Spoiled Home*? We chose *The Spoiled Home* because we felt that we were spending our free time buying items for our home or upgrading and decorating our house on the weekends instead of spoiling ourselves with manicures, pedicures, etc.

Do you have a mission or motto that directs your digital brand? "Work hard and be nice to people." Our motto from the beginning has always been to uplift and to be kind. There is so much negativity in the world, we hope that when people land on our page or discover our story, they find a bright spot where we can share not only some inspiration, but also a smile.

What do your followers walk away with after visiting your content platforms? With us, what you see is what you get. We do not think our houses are prettier than anyone else's. We do not think our marriages are more stable or our families more perfect. We hope that by sharing little snippets of our lives, pictures of our homes, and bargains that we find, that people can smile and be inspired and feel like they are connecting with friends. Because when all is said and done, it's our friendships and relationships with others that we want people to really value in life.

❂JULIET

Juliet Angus

est. 2013 | London, United Kingdom

When did you launch your site, julietangus.com?
In 2013, I was 36 years old and living in London. I had finished filming the first season of *Ladies of London* on Bravo and had also just stopped working in fashion PR as the TV show had become a full-time job. However, I knew I wanted to continue expanding my career in fashion while working on the show, and that's when I started my blog!

As much as I enjoyed being on a TV show, I couldn't come to terms with fully giving up my career in fashion. Starting a blog was my way of thinking ahead about my career beyond reality TV.

What has been the most challenging thing about being an influencer? You really have to be a modern Renaissance woman. You are your own creator, stylist, writer, editor, sometimes photographer, customer relations, PR, social media manager, booking agent, and more—all while keeping up the image that it's all done so seamlessly and effortlessly.

⊕NASTIALIUKIN

Nastia Liukin

est. 2012 | Los Angeles, California

What was life like before your influencer business? In the last chapter of my life, I was a professional athlete. I competed at the 2008 Olympic Games and won five Olympic medals. That truly gave me a platform to do what I love, which is inspire the next generation of young girls, whether they're athletes, entrepreneurs, or students. As such, I co-founded an app with my fiancé called Grander. It's a platform that connects young female athletes with professional mentors like myself and my Olympic teammates, college recruiters, sports psychologists, and more. We've started in the gymnastics arena and we plan to delve into other sports and female empowerment in general.

What inspired you to launch your influencer business? When I was competing in the Olympics, social media wasn't really a "thing." It was only after my gymnastics career ended that having this online presence and leveraging it for digital advertising opportunities became a viable career path. I realized that I had an organically built-in fanbase that trusted me, so authentically sharing my life with them, including what clothing I was wearing or coveting, where I was traveling, or what beauty products I was using, was a natural next step.

Is there anyone along the way that changed the trajectory of your business? I would say it's been the people around me: my fiancé, my family, and my team. They have always, always told me to stay true to myself and my passions. Whether that means what I choose to share on social media or what brands I choose to work with, they've always stressed the importance of being me.

What is one your favorite quotes? What does it mean to you? "Never quit on a bad day."

My mom told me this when I was a little girl and it has stuck with me forever. We will all have bad days and go through hard times, but it is so important not to give up or quit on those bad days.

What were you doing before you launched your influencer business? Before I started my blog, I was attending Utah Valley University studying communications and graphic design.

Has your blog always been called *Pink Peonies*? How did you decide on that name? My blog was and still is *Pink Peonies*. Pink has always been my favorite color and peonies have always been my favorite flower! I knew I always wanted to start some type of business and had that name in my head for when I did.

What inspired you to launch your influencer business? I originally started a blog as a way to document my life as a newlywed. It was more of a life journal for my family and friends to follow. Not long after I started my blog, our wedding was featured on the cover of *Utah Valley Brides* Magazine and that's when I started seeing more and more traffic to my little space on the internet. My wedding photos were being pinned and re-pinned on Pinterest and I started receiving fashion questions from women all over the country. They were more interested in what top I was wearing or what shade of lipstick I had on or what my husband, Drew, and I were doing that weekend. That's really what sparked the idea to change my focus and make *Pink Peonies* centered around the women who were following me and the way they could elevate their life through fashion, beauty, and decor!

Did anyone help you start your influencer business? When I started my blog, the only person who didn't think I was crazy was my mom. Day in and day out she would go out with me to take my outfit pictures. We would drive around and climb through trees and bushes to find the perfect location. She never complained, even when it was freezing outside! She could tell how much I loved it and she was so dedicated to helping me pursue something I loved so much. Years later, my good friend from high school admitted that all my peers had laughed at my blog and new business. I'm sure no one ever expected my blog and business to turn into what it is today. I'm lucky I had the support of my mom in the beginning.

How has having an influencer business changed your life? When I launched my blog, I never would have dreamed it would have grown so fast and large but, when it did, I knew it would be the perfect platform to help launch my childhood dream of having a clothing line. Today, I am a wife, mother of two babies, and I manage my two businesses—my clothing line, Rachel Parcell Collection and my blog, *Pink Peonies*.

◉RACHPARCELL

Rachel Parcell

est. 2010 | Salt Lake City, Utah

When did you start your influencer business? I was a new mom with a daughter that was less than a year old when I started my influencer business. I was 24, living in a small apartment while my husband was finishing up his degree in finance at BYU. We didn't have much back then, so my business served as an outlet for me to focus on fashion, something that I loved. I quickly learned that my little business was capable of growing to be much more, and it has since turned out to be an incredible blessing and adventure for me and my family.

Did anyone help you start your influencer business? As a new mom, I needed more than a little help to get my business going. My husband used to sneak away from class or work to take pictures, my mom would help with my daughter if I needed it, and all of my sisters were incredibly supportive! Finding content on a daily basis was challenging with everything we had going on back then, but all of those late nights writing and scheduling posts were worth it!

How did you come up with the name of your blog, *Ivory Lane*? Ivory is the middle name of both my husband and daughter, and I grew up on a street with the name Lane in it. My family is my inspiration for almost everything I do, so I wanted the name of my blog to reflect that is some way.

How has having an influencer business changed your life? It has allowed me to have a career in something that I love all while staying at home to be with my children. I would have never dreamed that all of this would be possible, so I absolutely cherish the opportunity I have been given.

Is there anything along the way that changed the trajectory of your business? My business has evolved naturally over the years just as my passion and interests have. I haven't fought that, which has always made the content that I generate fun and easy for me to do. Over the last couple years, I have found a passion for running and fitness, which I have incorporated into what has historically been a style/fashion business only.

❂EMILYIJACKSON

Emily Jackson

est. 2012 | Salt Lake City, Utah

⊛LIZADAMS

Liz Adams

est. 2011 | Chicago, Illinois

What was the inspiration behind your blog name, *Sequins & Stripes*? When I started my blog, I was 100% focused on fashion, fashion trends, and personal style. Sequins and stripes are two things I appreciate in my closet, so it just sounded right—it was catchy! Fast forward seven years and I'm married with two children and my content focuses heavily on lifestyle, but *Sequins & Stripes* will forever be how I started.

What inspired you to launch your influencer business? I studied textiles in college and worked as a clothing buyer for three years after school. I decided to completely switch careers and started *Sequins & Stripes* as a hobby to keep up with the fashion industry. I never dreamed it would turn into a full-time business!

Did anyone help you start your influencer business? I remember telling my dad that I wanted to quit my job and try to make my blog a full-time business and he was like "whattttt?" So, I wrote up a business plan and asked him to help me pay my rent for three months to see if this could work. I paid him back two years later, and now, years later, here we are! He was my first business partner.

What is one of your favorite quotes? What does it mean to you? "Your journey has molded you for the greater good, and it was exactly what it needed to be. Don't think that you've lost time. It took each and every situation you have encountered to bring you to the now. And now is right on time." - Asha Tyson

It's a reminder to enjoy the ride, take advantage of the opportunities that come to you, and don't compare your journey to someone else's.

"

Enjoy the ride, take advantage of the opportunities that come to you, and don't compare your journey to someone else's.

What inspired you to launch *Disco Daydream*? When I launched *Disco Daydream*, I was a stay-at-home mom who had just moved across the country away from friends and family. I wanted to create a space for myself to do something creative and connect with other people who shared the same interests as me.

What's the inspiration behind the name of your digital brand, *Disco Daydream*? I knew I wanted something that would hint to the bygone era that I often get inspiration from, and also something that sounded carefree and whimsical. To me, personal style is something that should be fun. Many of my looks are cultivated as a byproduct of daydreaming about things that inspire me (usually over coffee!) and I wanted my blog name to reflect that.

Looking back, is there any advice you would give yourself when you first launched your influencer business? When I first started blogging, I thought I needed to be just like other bloggers to be successful. I was afraid to try anything different than what was already out there. Now, I would tell myself that being different is a good thing. It is the constant reinvention that keeps me feeling inspired.

What is your favorite quote? What does it mean to you? "Your life unfolds in proportion to your courage."

I feel like a lot of who I am today is the result of being comfortable with being outside of my comfort zone. My husband and I have a "let's do everything" approach to life, which can be a little scary at times, but I have never regretted saying yes to big life decisions.

It is the constant reinvention that keeps me feeling inspired.

⊚DISCODAYDREAM
Lauren Johnson
est. 2015 | Dallas, Texas

What were you doing before you launched your influencer business? Prior to launching *Simply Sona*, I attended the Make-up Designory in Los Angeles and worked at MAC Cosmetics, which is where I gained most of my experience as a makeup artist. After eight months, I made the switch to a freelance artist. Then YouTube came along, and I fell in love with filming and editing videos—it was so therapeutic for me. I launched my YouTube in December of 2011.

How has having an influencer business changed your life? Being an influencer has definitely changed my life. As a YouTuber and influencer, I realized that social media offered me a powerful tool to connect with people around the world. Platforms like YouTube gave me the ability to engage in intimate conversations with my audience on a daily basis and find out exactly what they wanted from the beauty world. I have developed a community of amazing followers that trust and support me. And with that trust, I have been able to create my very own makeup line—Pérsona Cosmetics.

What do you wish you could go back and tell yourself when you first started? If I could go back, I would tell myself to "believe in yourself and go for it." I was always full of great ideas, but was too afraid to start them. Oftentimes, I thought my dreams were too big and I would convince myself out of pursuing them. It wasn't until I was in my mid 20s that I started looking at life differently and really understanding manifestation. I'm now a strong believer that no dream is too big as long as you believe in it and work really hard.

When I was 26, I ditched my traditional job and took a major pay cut to do what I love. I started my YouTube channel and worked really hard to build it to where it is today. While my friends were out socializing, I was in my room, filming and editing. Shortly after, I decided to start my own cosmetics line. Now, my products are being sold in Ulta Beauty and we're growing our brand so quickly. Always remember that your dreams are never too big! Believe in yourself and work hard in silence to make your dreams a reality.

⊗SIMPLYSONA

Sona Gasparian

est. 2011 | Los Angeles, California

⊚ COCOBASSEY

Coco Bassey

est. 2013 | Atlanta, Georgia

When did you launch your influencer business? Where were you at in life? I started my blog, *Millennielle*, in 2013 in Atlanta, Georgia. I had just finished grad school, and was between jobs, so I took the plunge! I always enjoyed reading online publications and my dream had always been to move to New York City to become an editor. With blogs starting to take off, I was able to pursue my dream in my own way—right at home!

What inspired you to get started? All the way back to my high school days, I had always wanted to create my own little corner of the internet. I taught myself the basics of web design, HTML, and CSS on MySpace. While everyone was talking about their "Top 8," I was designing and re-designing my page layout on a weekly basis! Blogging is the meeting point of so many of my biggest interests: graphic design, writing, photography, fashion—starting a business around that just felt natural to me.

Is running your influencer business your full-time job? Being a digital influencer is definitely one of my full-time jobs! I'm also a full-time product marketing manager for a global software firm. Even though there are days where my over-packed schedule drives me crazy, having a dual income gave me the flexibility to invest in my business from day one. Being a total brand and web design geek, I knew that building a strong digital brand wasn't cheap, so even on my busiest days, the hard work is worth it.

❖MONIKAHIBBS

Monika Hibbs

est. 2011 | Vancouver, British Columbia

What inspired you to begin creating and publishing digital content? I was inspired by my interests of home, family, entertaining, travel, food, and everything that was part of my everyday lifestyle. It was what came easy to me, and of course, what I was passionate about. I loved flipping through brand and lifestyle magazines, and knew I wanted to create something similar through my blog.

What was the name of your blog when you first launched in 2011? What is it called today? My blog's name when I initially started was *The Doctor's Closet*. Years later, I changed it to my name, rebranding as MonikaHibbs.com. Starting my blog as a new doctor, I wanted the name to reflect who I was, with a spin of my everyday lifestyle and interests. Since stepping away from medicine, I felt the need to change the name of my blog since numerous people would still ask what the "doctor" part meant. It is absolutely part of my story, however, it's also in my past. Developing a brand under my personal name just made sense.

What has been the most challenging thing about having an influencer business? A combination of balance, prioritizing, and the guilt of working too much...that includes mom guilt. I'm learning that I simply can't do it all. I've discovered that I do need help with not only my day-to-day business, but also with my kids and home obligations. Letting go and asking for help has been my biggest challenge, but, it has allowed me to be a better wife, mother, boss, and friend.

⚘INTERIORDESIGNERELLA

Jen Adams

est. 2016 | San Diego, California

What were you doing before your digital brand, I*nterior Designerella***? What inspired you to start?** I'm from a family that embraces our Hawaiian culture and I grew up hula dancing. So, while still in diapers, I was put in grass skirts and encouraged to dance my heart out! That was the beginning, friends! Through the years, I absolutely loved performing—it became an expression of gratitude and love with an audience and an opportunity to connect. I became fascinated with what makes others happy! Life is so full of joy, but it also has its valleys. I want people to know that through it all, they are loved. Our energy and the smiles we share impact people; they influence people.

I became a professional Polynesian dancer and instructor while finishing school. I loved it, lived it, breathed it—but it did not generate more than a side income. I always dreamed of having my own thriving business. Since I hadn't developed one yet, I was constantly trying out new ideas and failing forward while keeping my side entertaining hustle. My goal has been to provide an income that would allow my husband the opportunity to retire early to focus on his health. He has significant health issues and family is priority for me.

With a degree in psychology and an array of creative freelance work, I stumbled into the world of social media after much "encouragement"—AKA arm twisting, haha! There I was, a 32-year-old stay-at-home mom, still-aspiring entrepreneurial wife in sunny SoCal, and highly intimated by technology. I felt like a fish out of water, flopping around while trying to dive into the digital space—and loved it! It took me a year to figure out what I was doing. Then, once May 2017 rolled around...boom. Things suddenly changed and it became a real business.

Is there a single word that could sum up your influencer business? If I could only choose one word to sum things up, it would be "grateful"—yet that's an understatement. I am completely floored and honored to get to live out my dreams. I realize it could all be gone tomorrow—but while I'm here, with you, in these words, and on this page, I want to give thanks and take this opportunity to tell you that you are loved, your dreams matter, you can do it, and I'm rooting for you!

⊙LOMURPH

Lauren Murphy

est. 2014 | Dallas, Texas

When did you start your digital brand and why? I started my business in January 2014 at 23 years old. I was living in Dallas, working as a stylist, and completely unaware that this could lead to a full-time career. I knew I wanted a space where I could share my personal style, fashion tips, encourage women to try new things, dress for themselves, and feel their most confident!

What were you doing before you launched your career as an influencer? During and after college I was working as a wardrobe stylist on TV shows, in editorials, celebrity work, and for marketing campaigns. I never thought I would leave the styling world!

What has been the most challenging thing about having an influencer business? The most challenging part of having an influencer business is the many hats you have to wear on a daily basis. From editor, to accountant, to stylist, to creator, to manager. Everyday is different and brings new opportunities and challenges. Trying to juggle various roles, time manage, learn new skills, and attempting to "turn off" has been the most challenging aspect.

#LTKhome

Professional interior designers, master DIY decorators, and the forever hostess with the mostess, these inspiring home influencers keep every space in style.

◉ *anitayokota*
Anita Yokota
est. 2016 | Orange County, California

◉ *citrineliving*
Tamara Anka
est. 2014 | Saint Lazare, Quebec

est. 2015 | Cumming, Georgia
Kelley Nan Lopez
◉ *kelleynan*

◉ *chrislovesjulia*
Julia and Chris Marcum
est. 2009 | Rexburg, Idaho

Follow @liketoknow.it.home and check out
#LTKhome in the LIKEtoKNOW.it app to
discover all things home decor and design.

⊕ JOANDKEMP

Kemper Baugh

est. 2015 | West Monroe, Louisiana

How did your digital brand get its start? As soon as I came home with the idea of the blog, my husband Jordan did what he did best and started researching all of the ins and outs of starting a blog. With my love for fashion and his love for creativity, we knew it would be something we would love doing together.

What are the perks of having an influencer business? Being able to do something I'm so passionate about has brought complete joy to my life. Jordan and I absolutely love doing everything together, so this has just been something we have been able to add to the top of the list. It has also given us the much-desired opportunity to travel more. From the moment we met, it has always been a desire of ours to travel the world, and this job has been able to provide some incredible opportunities for travel and much more.

Is *Jo and Kemp* your full-time job? It is! It hasn't always been though. I was working as a stylist assistant for about a year while building my blog and brand. After that, I worked as a caretaker for my husband's grandmother for about a year and a half while continuing to build my brand. In January of 2017, I was finally able to take the blog full time and it's the greatest job ever! I never thought I would actually be able to make a living doing something I absolutely love.

EMILYANNGEMMA

Emily Ann Gemma

est. 2013 | Tulsa, Oklahoma

What were you doing before you launched your influencer business? Prior to blogging, I had just completed my Masters in Business in Arkansas, relocated to Virginia and worked for an IT company.

When did you start your blog, *The Sweetest Thing*? I started my blog when I was 24 for the purpose of journaling, more or less. I was living in Blacksburg, Virginia where my (now) husband was in his second year of medical school. My blog served as a 'diary' of our lives in Virginia because I had moved from my home state, Arkansas (15 hours away) and into a new apartment of my own with two female medical students. Blogging turned into a business for me in 2013. At that point, John and I had been married for one year and we were relocating monthly for John's medical school clinical rotations. We didn't have a steady income since we were moving from city to city each month. I began to realize that I could monetize my blog based on feedback from my growing number of followers who were no longer only family and friends. I would wake up, open my laptop and see dozens of emails from readers with questions regarding my hair, makeup, and clothing. It had never occurred to me that anyone would be interested, much less influenced by my hair, makeup choices, and clothing style. At this point, I knew I could turn "journaling" into a business.

Is your influencer business your full-time job? *The Sweetest Thing* keeps me busy and on my toes. Yes, it's a full-time job! And by full time, I mean more than forty hours per week. When my husband was in residency, there were many months where I was working more hours than him. In fact, he started helping me when he got home from the hospital.

How has having an influencer business changed your life? Wow! It's changed our lives incredibly. Going through medical school and residency is quite challenging for the student and spouse. John and I knew we'd be challenged physically (John's lack of sleep!) and emotionally (John and me, both!) but mostly, financially. It was a huge relief to have my business during those years, as I was able to not only provide for us, but also, start saving for our future.

What is one of your favorite quotes? What does it mean to you? My favorite quote is actually a Bible verse. It is Jeremiah 29:11, 'For I know the plans I have for you, plans to prosper you and not to harm you, plans to give you hope and a future.'

This is a verse that always and still does bring me so much peace. I grew up in a small town in Arkansas—a town with a population of 8,000. To be honest, I never in a million years expected for anyone to care about my favorite curling iron or mascara! When I began blogging as a job, I had my share of critics. I began to second guess myself often. I would always pray about it and ended up with so much peace. I knew there just had to be a reason that a small town girl like me was given the opportunity to share my interest in style and beauty with the world.

What were you doing before you launched your influencer business? I was working in marketing in the medical device field, specifically spine surgery. I traveled a lot and absolutely loved my job. I still love pursuing a career outside of my blog, so I continue to work as a consultant.

How did you come up with the name *9to5chic*? I love finding ways to express my personal style at work. I thought of it as a fun challenge: how can I bring "fashion" into this outfit while still being taken seriously during my presentation in the conference room?

What inspired you to launch *9to5chic*? When it launched, I had no idea that it would become a business. It was a passion project and I loved putting in the time without having any expectations of what could come from it. The influencer space was in its infancy—there were no brand partnerships with influencers and the idea of earning money while doing it was simply nonexistent.

What has been the most challenging thing about having an influencer business? I think the challenge for me is a universal one, whether I'm back at work in a more typical office or juggling the blog and consulting work: finding balance and being present in the moment. Multi-tasking has become a way of life. But I think to actually achieve the balance I'm looking for, I need to be able to give my full attention to one thing at any given time.

How has being an influencer changed your life? It completely changed my life. I have made changes in my career that I never thought I would make, for example, leaving the medical device industry—I hope to return one day! But the changes have been rewarding, allowing me the flexibility to build my own schedule and spend more time raising my young daughter. I am forever grateful.

◉ 9TO5CHIC

Anh S.

est. 2010 | San Francisco, California

I ended up dropping out of interior design school and quitting my job to become a full-time blogger and influencer...I'm pretty sure my grandparents aren't convinced that I have a job.

⊚ GOLDALAMODE

Cara Irwin

est. 2016 | Asbury Park, New Jersey

What were you doing before you launched *Goldalamode*? I was in school for interior design and working retail. I ended up dropping out of interior design school and quitting my job to become a full-time blogger and influencer. That's still a fun topic at family parties. I'm pretty sure my grandparents aren't convinced that I have a job.

How has having an influencer business changed your life? Having an influencer business has given me the freedom to create my own schedule. I struggle with chronic pain, so having this freedom has helped me live a happier and healthier life. It

has also allowed me to meet amazing people and learn so much about the industry.

Is there anything you wish you could go back and tell yourself before launching your influencer career? If I could go back I would tell myself to ask for help! When I first started, I was intimidated to ask seasoned influencers certain questions. I didn't want to sound stupid or lazy, but honestly, it's impossible and very time consuming to learn it all on your own. Reach out and grow with your community of influencers.

⊘ ALICIATENISE

Alicia T. Chew

est. 2011 | Washington, D.C. , United States

When did you launch your digital brand? What were you doing at the time? I started my blog in 2011 at age 21. I interned in New York at a couple major fashion houses in college, and when I returned back to campus, I wanted to stay connected to the fashion industry.

What inspired you to launch your blog, *Alicia Tenise*? I launched my blog because I loved fashion—my blog was my creative outlet and my way to share attainable style inspiration with like-minded girls my own age. As time progressed, I started to gain more followers, had the opportunity to partner with brands, and was able to monetize my passion project.

Is being an influencer your full-time career? My influencer business has turned into my full-time career. I've learned how to negotiate with brands, I have hired an assistant and a brand manager to join my team, and I've had the opportunity to use my creativity more and make some of my styled photo shoot concepts come to light.

What were you doing before you launched your influencer business? I was a restaurant designer at Cactus Club and Browns restaurants in Canada, and on a whim, I applied to be on *The Bachelor*! I got on the show, the experience was wild, and then somehow I landed the gig of being *The Bachelorette*. After that, my career as an influencer and TV host was born.

What inspired you to begin creating content as a digital influencer? I wanted to share my passion for style and decor with my followers who were always asking me where things were from. I love telling stories and sharing (*oversharing*), and my blog was a great outlet for me to do that!

Is your influencer business your full-time job? If not, what else do you do? No, it's part of it! I'm also a co-host of HGTV's *Love It or List It Too* and W Network's *Love It or List It Vancouver*. It could be my full-time job, but, I am proud to say JillianHarris.com has three full-time employees, and we are currently working on hiring our fourth!

How has having an influencer business impacted your life? It has allowed me to spend more quality time with my family while working from home, build a beautiful new home for our growing family, and employ three team members full time. There were challenges that I have learned over time to fix (ie. trying to fit photo shoots into every waking moment of the day and driving my fiancé, Justin, up the wall with photo requests). I've also learned how to deal with internet bullying. But for the most part, I love what I do, I love providing fun jobs, and I know that financially, we would not be where we are at now without the influencer business. I feel extremely lucky.

I love telling stories and sharing (oversharing), and this was a great outlet for me to do that!

⦿JILLIAN.HARRIS

Jillian Harris

est. 2010 | Kelowna, British Columbia

⊙MARTHAGRAEFF

Martha Graeff

est. 2012 | Miami, Florida

What were you doing before you launched your influencer business? I went to Central Saint Martins in London for six months after my studies in Brazil and after that, I knew I wanted to be in the fashion industry forever. Working as a buyer gave me a lot of knowledge about fashion and the relationship with the consumer. It was a major responsibility to travel around Milan, Paris, and New York to get the right merchandise for the store. This job taught me a lot. Choosing clothing for different types of women was a great experience, but I still felt the need to communicate with them. That's why I created the blog.

What inspired you to become an influencer? What inspired me the most was all of the different women I met along the way. Artists, designers, creatives, even my boss! I always liked to communicate and exchange tips about fashion, traveling, beauty, and health. Blogging was a perfect way to have this conversation, reaching people from different countries.

How has having a career as an influencer changed your life? It has given me financial support and it has opened many doors for other goals I have in life. The following I earned throughout the years has helped me spread the word about different charities and philanthropic work that are important to me, like the time I was able to share my visit to a Syrian refugee camp to raise funds for children's schools in India.

Is there anyone or anything along the way that changed the trajectory of your business? I started shooting for my blog by stopping people on the streets and asking them to take a picture! I did that for more than two years before I had the help of photographers. It was very interesting to have the view of someone who is not a professional behind camera. That made me more relaxed and it also taught me not to always feel dependent on a structured team. Today, I work with a team, but I still stop people on the streets sometimes to get a different perspective. It is a business, but I appreciate the naturality in the content.

⊛MACKENZIEHORAN

Mackenzie Horan Beuttenmuller

est. 2009 | Greenwich, Connecticut

When did you start your blog? I started my blog out of my sorority dorm room as a junior at Bucknell in 2009. I was 20 years old, reading a ton of blogs as a creative escape from my French literature classes, and decided to start my own blog to keep family and friends in the loop during my semester abroad in the Loire Valley. I loved the practice of daily writing and photography and stuck with it after I returned to the U.S.

Has your blog always been called *Design Darling*? Yes, my blog has always been called *Design Darling*, but the study abroad offshoot was appropriately titled *Mackenzie en France*, ha! I love interior design, personal style, and a good alliteration, so the name *Design Darling* felt just right.

How has being an influencer changed your life? In addition to giving me the freedom to do something I love and work from anywhere, the blogging industry has introduced me to several of my dearest friends. Three of my bridesmaids were friends I made through blogging!

Is there anything you wish you could go back and tell yourself at the beginning of your influencer career? Document everything! I didn't really get into original photography until a couple years into my blog, and now I love being able to look back at my first apartment in New York or a certain weekend in Nantucket.

What is one of your favorite quotes that keeps you going? My dad always says, "Just keep chipping away at it!" and I find myself repeating it any time I'm feeling overwhelmed.

✪ OHMYDEARBLOG

Brittany Robertson

est. 2013 | Grand Prairie, Alberta

What inspired you to launch *Oh My Dear Blog*?
I loved reading blogs and had always wanted to try starting one myself, but felt intimated by the process, and on top of that, I had no idea what I would blog about. My good friend, Kellsie, encouraged me to start one anyway and just share what I loved. I had no history with interior design prior to starting my blog or my Instagram account, however, it was through sharing photos of our home decor that my blog and social media channels took on a more interior design theme. I had such an overwhelmingly positive response to those photos, which encouraged me to share more of how I was decorating our new home and everything really started to take off from there.

Are there any decisions you made that you would attribute to the growth of your business?
I decided early on I was going to decorate with a more eclectic style because that's what I liked, and not worry if anyone else would like it. That ended up being what my followers were drawn to, and now I love being able to encourage everyone who wants to decorate their space to have fun, not to play by the rules, and express their own style!

What has been the most challenging thing about having an influencer business? The most challenging thing for me is styling photos, but it's also my favorite aspect as well. A lot of work goes into staging each photo and the amount of mess it creates is surprising, even to me!

⬡THESTYLEBUNGALOW

Stephanie Hill

est. 2014 | Palm Beach, Florida

What were you doing before you launched your influencer business? I was working in public relations and social media. Prior to that, I was a professional ballerina for a small company in West Palm Beach!

Did anyone support you in the launch of *The Style Bungalow*? I didn't do this alone! I asked friends in the advertising industry for advice on branding and design—I was very fortunate to bounce so many ideas off of them and use them as a sounding board the first couple of months after I launched my blog. I've also worked closely with the same photographer since the beginning! Her name is Chelsae Anne and she's been instrumental in helping me capture the overall mood and feeling of my brand through her beautiful imagery. I have also had a close support system with my friends here in Florida and my family in Texas.

Are there any important lessons you've learned in your career as an influencer? The start of 2018 had me thinking a lot about my blog, which led me to pump the breaks on creating content, do research, and pause. I thought, "Why am I doing this?" Sometimes as a creative person you're expected to know everything—what you don't take into account is life, which ultimately forces your style (and beliefs) to evolve. During this break, I read a quote from Leandra Medine that said, "you can't know your style until you know yourself…" From that point on, I vowed to focus less on fashion, trends, and the Instagram algorithm, and more on my story… my personal evolution to becoming the woman I am today, who is much more confident, free, and resilient than I ever could have imagined.

⊛KERRently

Courtney Kerr

est. 2011 | Dallas, Texas

What is your career background? How did it lead you into the influencer industry? Since the age of 16, I've worked in retail. It's in my blood and I love it...I always joked that I could sell anything to anyone. After getting my degree in Fashion Merchandising, my dream was to one day become the CEO of a large retailer. Throughout my 20s, I had the pleasure of working for some incredible brands. Leaving retail was never in the cards for me because it was all I really ever knew, but I truly believe that all those years working in a mall and dealing with customers prepped me for the career I have now as an influencer. Being a blogger, just like working retail in a mall, can be humbling at times... and ultimately, we are just e-commerce salesgirls!

Did anyone help you launch your influencer business? In August of 2011, I was on a reality show on Bravo called *Most Eligible: Dallas*. A good friend of mine, Amber Venz Box, had just launched rewardStyle two months prior and suggested that I start a style blog as a way to share all the looks I wore throughout the show. I truly had zero idea what I was getting myself into and didn't even own a laptop computer or camera at the time. The idea to start a blog spiraled into a full-time job as an influencer, a spinoff show called *Courtney Loves Dallas*, and countless brand partnerships and collaborations. Fast forward seven years...I probably owe Amber a really big thank you, don't you think?!

How has having an influencer business impacted your life? Being an influencer and having my own successful business has empowered me in ways that I never dreamed of. Doors have opened, relationships have been cultivated, and boxes have been checked. But the most rewarding thing is looking in the mirror everyday and feeling proud of what I do.

⊛IAMBEAUTICURVE

Rochelle Johnson

est. 2012 | Little Rock, Arkansas

How did you decide on the name of your digital brand, "*Beauticurve*"? I wrote down a bunch of names and let them "speak to me." I felt like "*Beauticurve*" was a great depiction of how I felt about myself and my curves. Curves are beautiful.

Is there a specific message you wish to spread to your followers? I really want to spread the message to love yourself, wherever you are in your journey to becoming your best self. Your value is not tied to the number on the scale or the size you wear. You're worthy to receive everything that is for you at whatever size you are right now!

Is there anything you wish you could go back and tell yourself before you launched *Beauticurve*? I wish I could tell myself not to sell yourself short. It took me a long time to understand my value! I also would have worked a little harder and smarter to establish my brand and voice—more intentional actions. I was not prepared for the growth.

Is there anyone along the way that changed the trajectory of your business? The first thing that comes to mind is my son. I worked really hard while I was pregnant and had some epic moments. What I thought would slow me down, actually boosted my entire business. Once my son was born, I feel like it forced me into full-time blogging and it allowed me to connect to my audience on a whole different level. Now my son is a part of my blog and he fits right in.

⬡ITSYBITSYINDULGENCES

Shannon Pulsifer

est. 2013 | Orange County, California

What were you doing before you launched your influencer business? I was both blogging and practicing as a licensed marriage and family therapist concurrently for the first three years of my influencer business. The idea for *Itsy Bitsy Indulgences* came about as I was working for a non-profit agency. The company was going through some shifts, I was feeling frustrated, and decided to start a blog as a creative outlet—a place where I could share and cultivate my interests outside of work. I would come home from work and spend the evenings editing photos and writing. It's funny how therapeutic it was for me to be able to share these other interests I had. It always surprises me how one place in your life can catapult you into a completely different space if we allow it to and trust the process.

Did anyone help you start your influencer business? My business actually began as a joint venture between my younger sister and myself (she ended up making a career change, which didn't allow her enough time to blog at the same time, so after two years, I took it on by myself). We shared the responsibilities of writing, taking photos, and post conceptualization. And my husband, TJ, has always been the photographer (bless him).

Has your blog always been called *Itsy Bitsy Indulgences*? The blog name is the same today as it was almost six years ago when it first launched. It came from a place of realizing that life is meant to be lived, enjoyed, and balanced out through those small indulgences: a designer handbag with a bargain pair of shoes, a night of sipping champagne and a morning spin class, working hard and traveling to disconnect—all those little indulgences that make life oh, so sweet!

Is your influencer business your full-time job? Yes, this is my full-time job along with being a mom. I feel so blessed to be able to wake up and do this on a daily basis. I still stay educated on mental health trends, as it's something I still incorporate on the blog, but I am no longer a practicing therapist.

Is there anything along the way that changed the trajectory of your business? Becoming pregnant completely changed the course of my business. I shared a lot of vulnerable and honest reflections about being pregnant and life as a new mom, which I think many people were able to relate to on a personal level. I was completely honest and raw in what I wrote. I saw tremendous growth, as well as an increased connection with my readers. Seeing how positively people responded to honest vulnerability (and sprinkled in sarcastic humor about life in general) encouraged me to continue to share, and in turn, connect with my readers.

...unless you ask for the things you want, you'll never get them!

⊙ CASSIESUGARPLUM

Cassie Freeman

est. 2005 | Dallas, Texas

What was life like when you launched *Hi Sugarplum*? I started *Hi Sugarplum* in 2005, before blogging was actually a "thing" and certainly before you could make a career of it! We had just moved from Nashville to Dallas and I had two young kids at home. The blog allowed me the space to be creative and connect with others without taking me away from my family. For the first year, I think the only readers were my family and a few close friends.

How did you choose that name? My grandfather was larger than life and always greeted me with a booming, "Hi, Sugarplum!" He was my whole world, so when I lost him in early 2005, I was drowning in grief. Soon after, I started *Hi Sugarplum* as both a distraction from the grief and a much-needed creative outlet. The name honors him and is now my happy little place on the internet where I share my life and passions with my readers who feel more like friends.

Is there anyone along the way who changed the trajectory of your business? Until three years ago, my husband and son had been taking all my photos…and usually in the alley behind our house! When I met Mary Hafner, everything changed—I've never used another photographer. Together we found the bright, happy style that defines my brand today. Those photos led to appearing on the cover of *Redbook* Magazine and ultimately designing my own line of clothing with Gibson Brand for Nordstrom!

Do you have a favorite quote or mantra? I always say, "It can't hurt to ask!"

Running your own business can be tough, especially as a woman. But unless you ask for the things you want, you'll never get them! And besides, the worst thing that can happen is they say, "No."

When did you start your blog *Mode & The City*? How did you come up with the name? I started blogging in June 2007. My blog was, and is still, named *Mode & The City*. Honestly, I can't even remember why I picked this name, but what is sure is that I never realized it would be such an important decision! I contemplated changing the name several times over the years, but in the end, decided to stick to it.

What inspired you to launch your blog in 2007? At the time, there were very few blogs in France. I was reading a few American blogs and thought it would be fun to give it a go myself but for a French audience.

What were you doing before you launched your influencer business? I was still a student. I then worked at Hermès for four years before quitting my job in 2014 to start blogging full time.

How has being an influencer changed your life? It gave me freedom and strength I would never have dreamed about having my own company or being my own boss one day, but I enjoy it tremendously. I even get the chance to work with my fiancé every day, as he joined the business in 2017. He has always been very supportive and instantly saw the potential. He gave me confidence that what I was doing mattered, even when I doubted myself.

❤DAPHNEMODEANDTHECITY
Daphné Moreau
est. 2007 | Paris, France

❦ ADDISONSWONDERLAND

Brittany Hayes

est. 2014 | Monroe, Georgia

What were you doing before you launched your influencer business? Prior to becoming an influencer, I was running a bedding company that I created and launched in July of 2011. I appeared on ABC's *Shark Tank* in February 2013 for my bedding line and my social media following began to soar.

What inspired you to launch your influencer business? In the summer of 2014, I was at a place where I wasn't sure what to do next. I had a great company and a growing social media following for my bedding company, but I was drowning in stress from juggling this manufacturing company and being a new mommy for the second time. I needed an outlet for my creativity and wasn't quite ready to completely put an end to *Addison's Wonderland,* so I turned it into my blog.

What's the most valuable thing you've learned from your career as an influencer? At some point, a few years into launching my blog, my husband, Mark, sat down with me and really stressed the importance of defining my goals and my path. Once you have an "end goal" in mind, it is much easier to understand which collaborations are worth taking and which are worth losing a little money on by declining. Defining my dream has steered me down the path of wanting everything I do and share to be authentic and in line with my overall vision for *Addison's Wonderland.*

Is your influencer business your full-time job? Yes, I am a full-time blogger. My husband and I also own three other construction businesses as well as a house flipping company. I use all of our adventures and renovations for blog content, so it comes together full circle.

⊛FASHIONEDCHICSTYLING

Erica Hoida

est. 2012 | Encinitas, California

What were you doing before you launched your digital brand? Before my blog, *Fashioned/Chic*, really took off, I was actually a personal stylist! That's where my love of fashion really began. My passion is helping people look and feel their best. I love styling, and I try to incorporate styling tips and tricks into my blog that hopefully continue to inspire people. When you look good, you feel good!

Did anyone help you start your influencer business? My husband, James, has always been my best business partner. He's a gifted photographer and has a knack for web design and editing, too. So we make a pretty good team!

What has been the most challenging thing about having an influencer business? I would say that the most challenging thing is maintaining balance in my life. It is easy to let the business become what my entire life revolves around. Life can just get so crazy! But I've learned to take breaks, to travel just for fun, to spend time with family, and to do things that re-center me and remind me of what's important.

What do you wish you could go back and tell yourself when you first became an influencer? Just go with the flow and breathe...

> There are always going to be a million reasons why you feel like you can't (or shouldn't) take a risk, but if you don't, you may be missing out on something amazing you didn't even know existed.

❂ SOMEWHERELATELY

Brooke Tredway and Meggan Bowlsby

est. 2013 | New York City, New York and Dallas, Texas

How did you two meet? We're both from Iowa. We met through mutual friends at a party in high school and instantly clicked.

What inspired you to launch your digital brand, *Somewhere, Lately*? We started *Somewhere, Lately* for fun, as a hobby. We love fashion and it was our creative outlet outside of our corporate jobs. We had dreams of it becoming a full-time career, but we had no idea how to even make that happen. Zero. It took a lot of time, a lot of trial and error, and a lot of learning, but we finally figured it out!

What do you wish you could go back and tell your younger *Somewhere, Lately* selves? Don't worry about pleasing anyone. Be yourself, unapologetically.

What is one of your favorite quotes? What does it mean to you? "Take the risk or lose the chance."

There are always going to be a million reasons why you feel like you can't (or shouldn't) take a risk, but if you don't, you may be missing out on something amazing you didn't even know existed.

✦JEANWANG

Jean Wang

est. 2010 | Boston, Massachusetts

What were you doing before you launched your blog, *Extra Petite*? I worked in financial services at one of the "Big 4" firms—it was my first job out of college and I was there for over six years. As a petite, more reserved woman in a male-dominated industry, I struggled to find confidence and didn't feel like I was being taken seriously. This ultimately inspired me to start my blog, and I began sharing how to gain confidence and how to put your best foot forward, despite height or stature.

My business started as a way of documenting my journey to build a wardrobe that fit well and gave me confidence. It's evolved from there, but the idea that style transcends size and can empower you in any situation has always been at the heart of it.

Did anyone help you start your influencer business? My husband (boyfriend at the time) was starting to get interested in photography, and the blog turned out to be a great excuse for us to buy our first DSLR camera. There was a camera store down the street that was having a going-out-of-business sale, and we bought a DSLR for a hundred bucks. It was loud, heavy, and took four AA batteries to run. There was definitely a learning curve, but learning it together while growing the business has made this journey all the more special.

Has your blog always been called *Extra Petite*? I cringe just thinking about this, but when I first started my blog it was called *gulp* … *Petite Asian Girl*. It was a terrible suggestion from my husband, who claims he was joking, but my naive self didn't give it a second thought and I went ahead and bought the URL.

The name *Extra Petite* represents my personal quest as a short, smaller-framed gal to find stylish clothing that fits. The name is a bit of a double-edged sword though, because it can be a turn-off to women who aren't petite or don't think they are. But the idea of finding clothes that fit and flatter your body type, and using personal style to inspire confidence in yourself—those are ideas that can appeal to anyone.

⊘ SHALICENOEL

Shalice Noel

est. 2014 | Los Angeles, California

What inspired you to launch *Shalice Noel*? I remember sitting at the edge of my bed, praying a desperate prayer, God I need to supplement our income, and I'd love to work from home, and it has to be a pretty special job because I have a houseful of children—and with that, I left that prayer and continued being a full-time mom. It almost brings tears to my eyes thinking about how grateful I was for my first check! I could stay home with my babies, share my love of fashion, and get paid. It's really special, and I don't take it for granted.

What were you doing before becoming an influencer? I was a full-time mom of four kids, ages ranging from one to six. Before that, I was an event planner.

What is one of your favorite quotes? What does it mean to you? "In order to be irreplaceable, one must always be different" - Coco Chanel

You have to keep it fresh and stay inspired. For me, that meant limiting my time scrolling on social media and starting a mood board; finding inspiration everywhere from the LA flower market and traveling, to my own children's style.

It was a unique time that I am forever grateful for because I really got to see who believed in me from the start.

⦿LIVVYLANDBLOG

Olivia Watson

est. 2014 | Austin, Texas

What were you doing before you launched your blog, *LivvyLand*? Prior to launching *LivvyLand*, I worked in the marketing department of a (now global) jewelry brand. It was a time when the company was growing rapidly but still fairly small. Thus, my role was a ton of different things. I worked on social media, the brand's fashion blog, copywriting for products, photography, videos—lots of different responsibilities that ended up being amazing preparation for the world of blogging.

What inspired you to launch your influencer business? When I worked in social media for the jewelry brand, we would collaborate with influencers all over the United States—a lot of whom were mothers who were able to run their own successful businesses and also be stay-at-home moms which totally blew my mind and introduced me to a concept that I would eventually aspire to create for myself one day. I watched my coworkers have babies and return to work with opportunities stripped away. I didn't want starting a family to become a career setback (which of course, it shouldn't be in the first place!), and thus, that was the driving force in creating my blog—to one day be a mom with a working business of my own.

Did anyone help you start your influencer business? When I launched my blog, I didn't have the funds or resources to hire a professional photographer but I did have the drive and passion to figure out how to make it work. This meant relying on friends and family to help me snap outfit photos. My coworker and I would take photos in an alleyway behind our office during our lunch breaks, my friends would take a photo of me up against the wall of my old apartment complex before heading to dinner, or my mom would come over and we'd drive to a random building and take rounds of outfit pictures. I'd change in the back of the car and she'd blast the air conditioning from the front—God bless her, the Texas heat is no joke!

I wasn't earning much money in the beginning and all extra funds went to clothing for posts, so I'd pay my friends and family in iced coffees or treat them to lunch after a shoot. It was a unique time that I am forever grateful for because I really got to see who believed in me from the start—before there was any success to my business.

What were you doing before you launched *A Pinch of Lovely*? I was a graphic designer for LSU Athletics right out of college, where I worked my way up to the creative director position. Turns out branding, photo-shoot planning, and having a creative eye are all things that I still use from my full-time job on a daily basis.

What was the inspiration behind the name *A Pinch of Lovely*? *A Pinch of Lovely* started as me sharing little bits of inspiration I found online. Once I started focusing more on fashion and lifestyle, it remained a relevant name from a branding perspective.

Is there any advice you would give to anyone wanting to start a career as an influencer? My main advice for anyone who wants to start an influencer career is to never stop learning! Read everything you can about tech, business, self-employment, photography, travel, creative writing, etc.

My main advice for anyone who wants to start an influencer career is to never stop learning!

❂ APINCHOFLOVELY

Krystal Faircloth

est. 2012 | Baton Rouge, Louisiana

Is your influencer business your full-time job? If not, what else do you do?
It is and it isn't. I like to say that I'm a full-time blogger and a full-time actress because I wake up every day and work on both. Sometimes the blogging work load is heavier, sometimes the acting work load is heavier but right now they are both full-time.

What is one of your favorite quotes? What does it mean to you? "Comparison is the thief of joy." - Theodore Roosevelt

Though this was written so long ago, this quote has never been more relevant. In the age of Instagram and curated feeds, I try to always remember that comparison only leads to insecurity and sadness. I try to focus on what I'm doing and what I want to do, rather than what others are doing. This helps me be more creative and proactive rather than sulk about not having enough followers or not working enough. Whenever people ask for my advice on blogging or acting I say, "Do *you*! And do it every day!" Work on your blog or craft and don't worry how others got there, instead find your own path.

What were you doing before you launched your influencer business? When pursuing an acting career you often have to have a "day job." Usually one that you hate. I didn't want to wait tables so I started styling. First, I worked as an assistant for my friend, Matthew Ellenberger, who at the time, was the Creative Director of American Eagle and Aerie. It was the best job! I would travel four times a year with them and help him style the models for their campaigns. Eventually, I went from an assistant for AE to a stylist for Aerie! In between AE/Aerie shoots I took on personal clients. I never wanted to be a celebrity stylist, but I *loved* helping everyday people with their style and wardrobe. I would do major closet overhauls with them, take them shopping, then create outfits and look books for them to use every day. It was a really fun gig but it was also exhausting and a ton of work. The blog transition was great because it was something I could do part time and on my own schedule, leaving me more time and opportunity to focus on my acting.

✿ GRASIEMERCEDES

Grasie Mercedes

est. 2011 | Los Angeles, California

*Everything doesn't have to
be perfect from the start. I
now know, as long as I do my
best, and stay true to myself,
my business will thrive.*

❂DECORGOLD

Jennifer Prock

est. 2015 | Houston, Texas

What was the inspiration behind your blog name, *Decor Gold*? "Decor" is for decorating and "Gold" is short for golden retriever. In 2015 we had four goldens! Two of them had been with us since they were young, but the other two were seniors we had recently adopted. Rescuing older dogs and giving them a wonderful last few years is another passion of mine. We all have more than one passion, and combining mine to form my business name just made sense. Our goldens make frequent appearances in my images.

Do you run your influencer business full time? *Decor Gold Designs* is my full-time business. Often, it takes up far more than 40 hours per week. To be honest, there are days when I open my laptop first thing in the morning and work until I fall asleep with it on my lap at night—but that's okay because I love every second!

How has having an influencer business positively impacted your life? *Decor Gold Designs* has changed my life in more ways than I can count! The truth is, I wasn't looking to add a full-time business to my life, but it has fit in perfectly. Owning my own business has given us the freedom to do the things we love, such as travel and decorate (and redecorate) our home. It has also inspired me to refine my decorating and styling skills.

Is there anything you wish you could go back and tell yourself before you launched *Decor Gold*? If I could go back to the beginning when I started my journey, I would tell myself to slow down. My husband used to remind me that my business is a marathon and not a sprint. There is no rush. Everything doesn't have to be perfect from the start. I now know, as long as I do my best and stay true to myself, my business will thrive.

What were you doing before you launched _Hello Fashion_? I had just graduated from college, was working as an assistant manager at Aldo Shoes, and was really trying to find something I was super passionate about when I decided to start _Hello Fashion_. I also launched my online store, ILY Couture (now Shop Hello Fashion) within a couple months of starting my blog.

What inspired you to launch an influencer business? I was a huge tomboy growing up, but once I hit high school I was obsessed with fashion. I applied to a couple fashion design schools and was rejected, so I was looking for an outlet to really share the things I was passionate about. Blogging allowed me to be in control of what I was creating and to share the things I loved.

Is there anyone along the way that changed the trajectory of your business? I couldn't do this without my husband and my team. Once I started growing, I realized I needed a team to be able to make it more scalable. Our first employee, Whitney, started out as a part-time assistant and now, years later, manages the rest of the team—I 100% couldn't do it without all of her help. My husband helps me so much, too! Having quality people that can handle the day-to-day is what allows you to focus on the creativity and building the brand.

Do you have any words of wisdom from your own experiences? Always look for opportunities after rejection. If I hadn't been rejected from fashion school, I probably wouldn't be doing what I am today. I really believe that when one door closes, another one opens and that when you are pursuing the things you love because they are your passion, you will succeed in whatever you do.

❂HELLOFASHIONBLOG

Christine Andrew

est. 2011 | Salt Lake City, Utah

est. 2016 | London, United Kingdom
Erica Matthews
⚙ *ericafmstyle*

#LTKbeauty

From fishtail braid tutorials to creating the
perfect party pout, these makeup artists,
hairstylists, and influencer beauty gurus
always share the best new go-to glam.

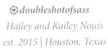

⚙ *doubleshotofsass*
Hailey and Kailey Nouis
est. 2015 | Houston, Texas

⚙ *lindseyreganthorne*
Lindsey Regan Thorne
est. 2009 | Charlotte, North Carolina

est. 2011 | Los Angeles, California
Sona Gasparian
 simplysona

est. 2013 | Fort Worth, Texas
Katey McFarlan
 kateymcfarlan

 andeelayne
Andrea De Silva
est. 2009 | Orange County, California

Get the best #LTKbeauty trends, tips, and
tricks on the LIKEtoKNOW.it app.

Having my own influencer business has been a dream job come true. I call the shots and have the chance to see the world...

What inspired you to begin creating content as a digital influencer? I wanted to have a reason to dress up again—I was always the most fashionably daring in high school and college, and I was proud of it! I also wanted a reason to get out of my house and office, where I was working as a graphic designer and web editor for an online software company. I felt cooped up. I knew getting out to shoot and enjoy the weather and my sister's company would be a welcome change. I wasn't sure what I was doing or what my goal really was in the beginning, so I was lucky my youngest sister was around to photograph and support me.

How did you decide on the name of your digital brand, *Hapa Time*? I called my blog *Hapa Time* because I actually didn't plan on centering it around fashion. Growing up, and even in college, I had planned to work for a women's lifestyle magazine. I wanted to write blog posts on beauty, food, fitness, art, and fashion. I'm "hapa"—which means half Asian—and essentially, I just wanted my blog to be a general representation of me. Over the years, my blog went from totally fashion focused to taking on more of a lifestyle approach, but the name still represents me even more so now!

How has having an influencer business positively impacted your life? Having my own influencer business has been a dream job come true. I call the shots and have the chance to see the world—something I never expected or even wanted. But now that I am traveling the world, I am so grateful!

❂ HAPATIME

Jessica Ricks

est. 2012 | San Francisco, California

The most challenging part is to always be in evolution, never stay on what you know, try to always go further.

◉ NOHOLITA

Camille Callen

est. 2014 | Paris, France

When did you start your digital brand, *Noholita*? I started my blog in January 2014. I was 23 years old and I was living in Bordeaux, a city in the south of France.

How did you come up with the name *Noholita*? I lived in New York for a year and there is a district called Nolita—I love that name and always told myself that if I had a baby one day I would name her that name. I mixed it with Soho, the shopping district in New-York, and *Noholita* was born.

What were you doing before you launched your influencer business? I was a communications student doing an internship at a bank. The webmaster of the bank actually helped me create my blog!

What has been the most challenging thing about being an influencer? The most challenging part is to always be in evolution—never staying with what you know, trying to always go further.

I can honestly say I work more now than I ever have in my life, but it never actually feels like "work"...

❂ OLIAMAJD

Olia Majd

est. 2014 | San Diego, California

What were you doing before you launched your influencer business? I actually went to college at San Diego State University and got my degree in accounting! I was lucky enough to have an offer as a full-time salaried accountant after graduating but, unfortunately, only one year in, I realized it was not a true passion of mine. I always had a passion for all things beauty so after two years as an accountant, I followed in my mother's footsteps, got my esthetician license, quit my accounting job, and then went to work full time with my mother in San Diego. That was where I developed a love for helping people, giving tips, and shortly after had the idea of starting a blog. I juggled the two for about two years and the rest is history!

What inspired you to launch your blog? I speak about this all the time on my blog, *Love, Olia*, but I truly believe it is so important to be passionate about what you do in life. I never started my blog as a way to make money or have it be my career. In fact, I never even thought that would be an option. I purely did it because I wanted a way to connect with others and share tips I had as an esthetician along with my love for beauty and fashion!

How has having an influencer business changed your life? My business has helped me instrumentally in all aspects of my life. I can honestly say I work more now than I ever have in my life, but it never actually feels like work. I've been able to buy a place for myself, learn discipline, and travel more than I could have ever dreamed.

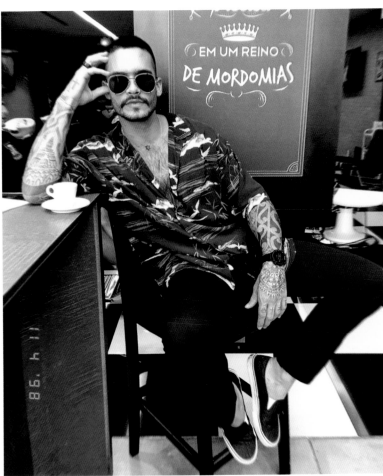

❂RHELDEN

Rhelden Nogueira

est. 2016 | São Paulo, Brazil

When did you start your influencer business?
I started my influencer business in the middle of 2016 when I was 25 years old. I was living, and still live, in São Paulo—the heart of Brazil in my opinion.

What were you doing before you launched your influencer business? Before I launched my influencer business I worked as a visual merchandiser at Armani Group, Boutique Chanel, and Nike. After that, I made three editorials for *Casa Vogue* inspired by fashion designers like Yves Saint Laurent, Issey Miyake and Alexander McQueen. During my career, I always worked as a fashion consultant and stylist—this is something that I never stopped doing.

How has having an influencer business changed your life? Being an influencer has helped me in all kinds of ways. My influencer career helped me become an ambassador of many brands that I never thought were possible. I'm so grateful for everything that is happening in my life and even more grateful for my followers because they are the most important part of it.

It has become an online community and I like to think of it as the modern-day village.

❂PUREJOYHOME

Liz Joy

est. 2013 | Connecticut, United States

What inspired the name *Pure Joy Home*? I chose this name because, at the time, my blog was really focused on being a new "homemaker." I was a fresh mom and learning how to cook, decorate, and even clean. Our last name is Joy, so I wanted that to be a part of it—and so *Pure Joy Home* was born.

How has having an influencer business changed your life? Oh wow, so many ways. Aside from my family, it is the reason I jump out of bed in the morning. I can't wait to get up and start chatting with my followers, sharing what I'm using, what I'm wearing, opening up the dialogue with them. It has become an online community and I like to think of it as the modern-day village.

The flexibility this career has given me is everything. I have been able to raise my kids at home while working on something I love. I don't think it gets any better than that, it's the balance we all want and somehow, I landed it.

What has been your biggest challenge with having an influencer business? It's the wild west out here. This is a very new way to market, and I guess learning as I go has been the biggest challenge.

What do you wish you could go back and tell your pre-*Pure Joy Home* self? Don't stress, be you, stay consistent, and the opportunities will come. Slow growth is the best growth.

Is there anything else you do other than your influencer business? I have always loved fashion and photography so I started posting lots of #ootds on Instagram (before Instagram was a thing) and naturally gained a following. People would always ask me about outfit details and a few kept requesting that I start a blog. I hadn't even read a blog at that time, but then I started following bloggers like *Song of Style* and *Sincerely Jules* and was so inspired by them. Starting a blog was still on back burner for me until I had a dramatic lifestyle change (moving from the city to a small lake town). I needed a hobby and a creative outlet which led to finally starting my blog. It started purely as a hobby, and I had no intention of turning it into a business, but that little decision to start a blog changed my life forever and I am so grateful for it!

I have been running *Gypsy Tan* full time since 2017! I also own a small tanning and accessories boutique but I have girls working for me to help run the salon.

How has having an influencer business changed your life? Becoming an influencer is life-changing in every aspect. It can never be compared to working for others. It consumes me, sometimes in a good way, sometimes not. My business is on my mind 24/7, but the beauty is that I love what I do, so I am blessed. It has given me the chance to travel to places and work for brands I never would have imagined. I am able to save for a home and future family!

✿ GYPSYTAN

Sabrina Tan
est. 2014 | Seattle, Washington

⊛EMILYMEN

Emily Men

est. 2015 | Los Angeles, California

What led you to become an influencer? Since I left school, I've never strayed from the fashion industry, but I've worked in many different areas within it. I've worked with celebrity stylists Joey Tierney, Rachel Zoe, and Brenda Cooper. I've also worked in the design department for 3.1 Phillip Lim and the accessories closet at *Elle*. Everything happens for a reason. Looking back now, I realize every step you take is a step toward something else. I wouldn't be where I am today without the experiences and relationships I cultivated in my prior jobs.

As far back as I can remember, I have used fashion as a way to express myself. I love that something as simple as what you are wearing can tell everyone who sees you so much about you. Early on in my career I stayed behind the scenes, first working in the wardrobe department for a TV show, and later, in celebrity styling. Starting a personal style blog seemed to be a natural extension of what I was already doing.

How did you decide on the name of your blog? My brother and I initially launched the *The Wardrobes* together—we wanted to have a gender neutral name that could include looks from both of us. The blog still has separate "His Wardrobe" and "Her Wardrobe" sections.

If you could go back in time and give yourself one piece of advice before you launched your digital brand, what would you say? Always trust your gut and be fearless! In the beginning, my biggest challenge was my own fear and lack of confidence holding me back—it's hard to make the shift from behind the camera to in front of it! This is something I'm still working on and I'm still not used to it!

⊚ A_SOUTHERNDRAWL

Grace Wainwright

est. 2011 | Louisville, Kentucky

What inspired you to launch your digital brand, *A Southern Drawl?* Honestly? The need to connect with others. I had transferred to a new school and was buried in coursework studying biomedical engineering. I didn't know a lot of people at the time and I sought to connect with people. I had always been interested in evolving my personal style, so I focused on fashion at the time.

How has your influencer business changed your life? I began my influencer business at a crucial time in my life. I had quite the fork in the road when I was graduating with my Masters of Engineering degree. Do I go the engineering route or do I take a risk and try to do this business full time? In the end, sharing my personal style, connecting with others, and creating inspirational content is what I am passionate about. It has even led me to create my fitness page, FitWithASD, and I now love being able to connect with people on a fitness level. It brings me so much joy to have the opportunity to inspire people to become a healthier version of themselves!

What is one of your favorite quotes? What does it mean to you? "If opportunity doesn't knock, build a door." - Milton Berle

It resonates with me in every aspect of my life, but especially in this industry. A passive approach to life will leave you by the wayside. Pursue your goals and dreams with unmatched passion and confidence.

✿ ASHLEYROBERTSON

Ashley Robertson

est. 2012 | Dallas, Texas

What do you enjoy most about having an influencer business?
Running a business means I get to be my own boss and funnel
my creativity and energy toward what I'm most passionate
about: to teach, empower, and connect a community of modern
women on a relatable and personal level by sharing beautiful,
curated content on noteworthy moments of fashion, beauty,
lifestyle, and entrepreneurship.

**Did anyone help you launch your influencer business? What
were you doing before you got started?** It was a hobby that
my husband, Austin, and I started together back in 2012. His
background is in IT and this was a creative project we started
when we got married. Before my influencer business, I was a
first grade teacher.

**What advice do you have for anyone looking to follow in
your footsteps?** So many things! Know your reader, but know
yourself first. If you are talking to everyone, you are talking to
no one.

**What is one of your favorite quotes? What does it mean to
you?** "The world is your oyster."

This quote means a lot to me. It was the sign I had hanging in
my classroom as a way to encourage and inspire my students
to never give up and keep working toward their goals. It also
was the sign my sister-in-law gave to me for my birthday and
inspired me to take our business full time.

Stepping out of your comfort zone, starting your own business, putting yourself out there to the world, it can be scary.

✪ STEPHSTERJOVSKI

Steph Sterjovski Jolly

est. 2012 | Toronto, Ontario

Has having an influencer business changed your life? My influencer business has been a huge blessing and opened so many professional opportunities that I'll forever be grateful for. It has grown and enabled my husband to join my business full time—we are able to work from home, travel, and create together. I still have to pinch myself that this is our life!

What has been the most challenging thing about being an influencer? Having your own business comes with its own set of challenges. The pressure is all on you. You are your own boss and there's a lot of accountability that is required to be sustainable. It can also be tough to "shut off" because you can work every hour in the day—there's always something that can be done. Sometimes I envy the 9 to 5,

but I wouldn't trade my job for anything in the world! I feel incredibly grateful. It's also helped us learn how to structure our lives and carve out time for things that matter most.

What is your favorite quote? Why does it resonate with you? "Most of our decisions are driven by either love or fear. Figure out who's doing the talking then decide what you'll do." - Bob Goff

Stepping out of your comfort zone, starting your own business, putting yourself out there to the world—it can be scary. I've always wanted my decisions to be out of love and not fear, so if I ever feel scared, I let myself feel it and do it anyway. If I listened to fear (and let it stop me from doing things), I probably wouldn't have the life I have today.

❀ CHAMPAGNEANDMACAROONS

Tamara Waterston

est. 2015 | Minneapolis, Minnesota

Don't be afraid to do what you really want to do with your life

What inspired you to launch your influencer business? It is a long story, but it was after I had a lump removed from my breast. I was sitting in bed and I remember texting my husband (while on pain pills) that I was going to make the blog something. I had launched it earlier that year and just sort of left it hanging. It was not a focus or a priority, and I knew that I had more to give to it and more to share. I have always been creative and drawn to creative jobs. The timing felt right and things started to happen. It is not an overnight success story by any means and I am still learning to this very day.

What have you gained from life as an influencer? Flexibility has been the biggest gain I have had from my blogging career. Being your own boss and setting your own goals, business dreams, and really making your life your own is beyond rewarding. Some days I can feel the creativity almost oozing out of me and other days I would like to close the blinds and climb back in bed with a giant sign that says, "Closed for business, come again!" You learn what works, and like anything, with time, you grow and the business grows.

Don't be afraid to do what you really want to do with your life. I was in a really dark and unhappy place with work and love before this whole world ever came about. I needed to do the work on the inside before I could move forward with anything else, and once I did, it made all the difference. Just remember that you are worthy of following your dreams. It won't all be perfect. It might look that way but trust me, it is all a little messy! You can do it. It might be small or grand, but whatever it is, make it yours!

What inspired you to become an influencer? When I started my blog, the term influencer was not around. Nobody was doing it as a full-time job, just as a hobby and to be part of a community of people who were passionate about fashion. I was always very into clothing. My mom had a really cool clothing label in the '80s and she also modeled in Tokyo, so she was really knowledgeable about Japanese designers like Yohji Yamamoto and Comme des Garcons. She also has collected vintage her whole life. I started collecting vintage when I was 10 years old. I didn't really fit in in the Texas suburbs, but I made friends online by blogging my outfits and writing about the collections and designers I admired.

How has being an influencer changed your life? That's a funny question because it has been my whole life since I was a teenager. I got to see blogging evolve and become the big business it is now. I always wanted to be an entrepreneur and I find running my own business extremely fulfilling. I also get to work with my husband, Jeff, who is a photographer and web developer. The web side of my business is extremely important, and he's been able to develop my website to maximize its income potential and usability for my readers. Having him is a real godsend.

What has been the most challenging thing about having an influencer business? I have been running my blog for 11 years, and sometimes I get burnout syndrome. It's hard work, and you have to be constantly inspired and evolving. I have to challenge myself to reach for new material that constantly inspires me and spurs my creativity. This cycle can be difficult, but it continues to push me outside of my comfort zone and I've learned to love it as part of my creative process.

Do you have any tips for budding entrepreneurs? Whether you want to be a blogger or develop your own products, it's really important to have a web and social presence. Educate yourself on how to build these effectively and start now. When you are constantly creating engaging content that improves your readers or customers lives in some way, you build a really engaged readership and customer base. I find the relationship I have with my readers really rewarding, and it always pushes me to keep growing.

✪ SEAOFSHOES

Jane Aldridge

est. 2007 | Dallas, Texas

❂ STEPHTAYLORJACKSON

Stephanie Taylor Jackson

est. 2015 | Dallas, Texas

What were you doing before you launched your digital brand? Prior to starting stephtaylorjackson.com, I worked in big box retail for nearly seven years. In addition to working full-time, I was working on my MBA at Texas Tech University. In 2014, I originally launched a little girls' luxury clothing boutique and I had a blog linked to my business. After doing the boutique for just under two years, I realized that my passion was for styling and creating content for women like me, and I changed course, re-branded, and re-launched as a fashion blog.

What was the inspiration behind your blog? I have always been a writer. I studied journalism in college and had a fashion blog that I curated and spent a lot of time on, but life happened after I graduated—I got married, had children, started working, and then

before I knew it, I hadn't written a fashion post in over eight years. The inspiration for my blog came from being burned out at work, and knowing that deep down, this is not what I was meant to be doing. I was yearning for something that I was passionate about. I was inspired by the empty feeling I had when I left work every day and I was determined to set out to do what makes me happy.

How has your influencer business changed your life? My business has changed my life in so many ways. I have been afforded so many incredible opportunities that, honestly, sometimes I have to blink and make sure I'm not dreaming. I feel so blessed to be able to contribute immensely to paying off student loans, paying for family vacations, and my children's education and extracurricular activities.

❂ ALYSON_HALEY

Alyson Haley

est. 2013 | Atlantic Beach, Florida

What made you decide to start your influencer business?
I started my blog back in 2013, when I was 27, after moving back home to Florida from Denver, Colorado where I lived for a year. During my time in Denver, I wasn't exactly welcomed with open arms by some of the people I had met in the circle of friends I found myself in. It was a time in my life where I had never felt more surrounded by people, yet so alone at the same time. So, as I was sifting through and dealing with the feelings of rejection that my time in Colorado left me with, I decided to focus on things that I really enjoyed and brought me fulfillment and happiness.

I had grown to love sharing my interests in shopping and personal styling through my posts on social media. I had grown to love interacting with the women who discovered my account through those posts, all of whom had similar interests as me. I had become increasingly intrigued by the idea of starting a blog, which was consistently requested by so many of these women. I thought it was a great idea and it also seemed pretty fun! I have always had a bit of a knack for the creative side to things, and thought, why not?

What was your career before you launched your blog?
I worked as a nurse for five years with experience in general neurology and neurosurgery, orthopedics and trauma, and eventually, progressive neurosurgery and neuroendovascular surgery before leaving the nursing profession in January 2015.

Has having an influencer business changed your life?
Completely! It has provided me with flexibility to be there for my friends or family on any given day. It has afforded me the ability to work from anywhere in the world, which has, in turn, helped me discover my love for travel. It has allowed me to be there for people who are struggling with the same things I've walked through in life, whether that be the loss of a parent or feelings of rejection. It's also given me the opportunity to inspire people to feel good about different aspects of their life, whether that is what they wear that day or traveling to a country they've never been to. I'm so thankful for all that my business has given me and allowed me to give to others so far. I can't wait to see what is next!

Are there any decisions you made along the way that changed the trajectory of your business? Hiring my assistant, Justine, in 2016 was an absolute game changer! Her hard work and willingness to take tasks off my plate has made room for me to invest more of my time into my blog posts, expand into different verticals, maintain a better work/life balance, and spend time dreaming up new ideas. She believes in and respects what I am trying to achieve through the blog for my readers. I firmly believe that my business wouldn't be where it is today without Justine by my side.

⚙FASHION_JACKSON

Amy Jackson

est. 2013 | San Diego, California

When did you start launch *Fashion Jackson* and what were you doing before you launched it? I started my influencer business in 2013 when I was 29, living in Dallas, Texas. Before, I was working full time for JCPenney headquarters as a sourcing manager for women's apparel.

Has your blog always been called *Fashion Jackson?* My blog has always been called *Fashion Jackson*. I knew I wanted my name to be a part of it. After a few days of brainstorming and writing down hundreds of ideas, as soon as I thought of *Fashion Jackson*, I knew that was the one!

How has having an influencer business changed your life? In the beginning, it started as just a fun hobby, but after a year, I noticed I would be able to turn it into a business in the near future. After a lot of planning and goal-setting, I was able to leave my full-time career of seven years to pursue my passion.

What was life like before _Stylin by Aylin_? I worked in the interior design industry designing residential, commercial, and model homes. Then, I left that career to pursue my own handbag line which was a great experience—I hope to have my own line again in the near future! I then left my design jobs to pursue being a full-time, stay-at-home mom to my two precious kids!

What was the inspiration behind _Stylin by Aylin_? To be very honest, prior to my blog I had lost a part of who I once was. There were days I would feel depressed, not knowing why—those bad feelings would then turn into huge guilt. After some soul searching I came to realize that I had lost my creative side, and as a result, had lost my identity. Having this blog and the ability to inspire and help people through using my creativity has been life changing. _Stylin by Aylin_ has made me a better mother, wife, sister, daughter, and friend. I sincerely thank all of my followers so much for their support, and for following the journeys that are yet to come. It means more to me than they know.

Has your life changed since becoming an influencer? Having this business has changed my life for the better! To be able to support my family and help others by pursuing my dreams is more than I could have ever wished for. Having a place to share my creativity is my favorite part about the job. It's so important to love what you do.

Having a place to share my creativity is my favorite part about the job. It's so important to love what you do.

⊚ STYLINBYAYLIN

Aylin G.

est. 2014 | San Diego, California

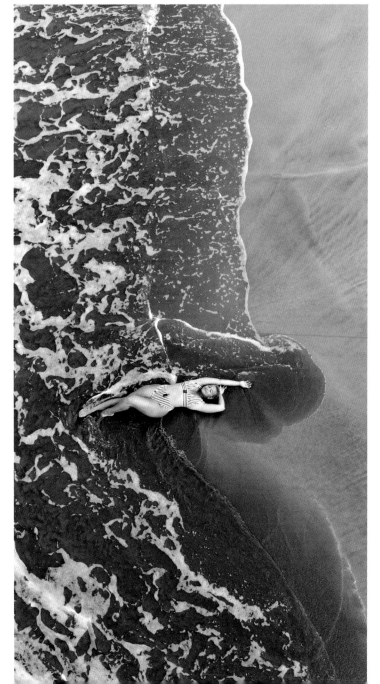

⬠LAURENELYCE

Lauren Price

est. 2012 | Atlanta, Georgia

What were you doing before you launched your influencer business? I was working as an assistant account executive at a PR firm in Washington DC. I majored in public relations and communications and was supporting media relations and social media strategy for some of the firm's multicultural accounts.

Has your blog always been called *Lauren Elyce*? I started my blog under the name *Fashionably Lo*. My nickname growing up was Lo and because I was starting out solely with affordable fashion and style, I liked the idea of a play on words. Lo=low/affordable price points. In 2017, I decided to change the name of my blog to *Lauren Elyce*— my first and middle name. Over the past few years, my focus shifted from just fashion to include personal style, travel, beauty, home, and more. I wanted a name that could easily transform with my focus and direction over time and what better way to do that than with a blog named after me.

How has having a digital brand changed your life? Having my own business as an influencer has changed my life in so many ways. Not only have I been able to focus in on my passion for creativity but I also now have the flexibility to spend more time with friends and family, travel to new and exciting places, and follow other passions of mine. It gave me the courage and the confidence to start a new business and constantly explore new opportunities to expand my brand as a businesswoman.

What do you wish you could go back and tell yourself? Identify your brand and niche. When I first started blogging, I knew my focus would be affordable fashion. Surprise: that isn't a niche. There are thousands of affordable fashion bloggers all doing amazing things and if I could go back in time, I would spend more time identifying the things that would make my affordable fashion blog unique. Now, over time, I've been able to pinpoint my perspective, point of view and the things that make me stand out aesthetically, personally, and with my storytelling. The moment I put a focus on those areas of my business, I noticed a huge increase in engagement, brand partnerships, and exciting opportunities.

What is one of your favorite quotes that you live by? I don't think this is necessarily a famous quote but I love to live by: Be you! In an industry that can be full of comparison, maintaining that true sense of self is something I try to live by on a daily basis.

⊚DRIVENBYDECOR

Kris Jarrett

est. 2011 | Connecticut, United States

How did you choose the name *Driven by Decor* for your blog? My blog has been called *Driven by Decor* since day one. I chose the name because it reflected my passion for home decor and also because I would, quite literally, drive around to stores finding the best home decor deals for my readers.

What were you doing before you launched *Driven by Decor*? I started *Driven by Decor* while also caring for my two daughters and working part time as a prenatal and cancer genetic counselor. Life was pretty crazy-busy—after getting my girls ready for school and on the bus in the morning, I'd hop in my car to go to work, get home right before the bus pulled up to drop them off, and then spend time with my family until after my girls' bedtime, when I would finally have time to work on *Driven by Decor*.

I never imagined that I wouldn't return to my genetics career after a couple of years, but *Driven by Decor* ended up growing so much and being so rewarding and fulfilling that I never went back.

What is your biggest challenge with running an influencer business? As crazy as it may sound, one of my biggest challenges is setting limits on the time that I spend on my influencer business. Unlike my job in genetics where I left the work behind the second that I walked out of the office each day, when you have your own business, there's always something that you could be working on. I'm my own worst boss when it comes to what I expect to achieve each day!

When you get to work on something you love it's a blessing. But when you get to work with people you love it's truly a gift.

❖ ALIFEDOTOWSKY

Ali Fedotowsky-Manno

est. 2014 | Los Angeles, California

What were you doing before you launched your influencer business? Before I got involved in the entertainment business and writing my blog, I actually worked at Facebook. I was an account manager for online advertisers. I loved that job so much. I still miss it at times! But I chose to leave that job to find love on TV! I don't regret my decision for a second, but it was certainly a very difficult one to make at the time. After Facebook, I went on *The Bachelor* and then *The Bachelorette* which led to hosting my own travel TV show called *1st Look* on NBC. Since then, I've worked as a correspondent on *E! News* and now I am currently a regular on the show *Home & Family* on Hallmark Channel.

Has your blog always been called *Ali Luvs*? Yes, I choose that name when I started it in 2014 and it just sort of stuck. I've thought about changing it multiple times but ultimately decided to keep it. It is, after all, a blog about all the things I love and I am passionate about, so it works!

How has having an influencer business changed your life? Starting my blog has completely changed my life in every way. It has allowed me and my husband to buy a beautiful home in Southern California. It has allowed me to work from home three days a week so I can raise my children. And each and every day I get more and more inquiries from businesses wanting to work together. My dream for the future is to start a clothing line for the everyday girl that's cute and affordable!

Is there anyone along the way that changed the trajectory of your business? My photographer, Ashley Burns, has been a part of my business since August 2016 and, since then, I really feel like my blog has gone from a hobby, to making a little extra cash, to a full business. Working with Ashley has made my content look more professional which I believe resulted in more people following me on social media that didn't know me from TV. She has helped me work smarter, not harder, and has become a really great friend. She helps me brainstorm new content ideas and in general just makes working on my blog more fun! I think when you get to work on something you love it's a blessing. But when you get to work with people you love it's truly a gift.

What inspired you to launch your influencer business? I was working in a very business environment as a key account executive in health science without a lot of creative freedom. I decided that writing a blog couldn't be too difficult, so I simply got a template off of WordPress and figured it out. My husband, Charles, and my cousin, Jillian Harris, both encouraged me!

Has your blog always been called *Fraîche Nutrition*? Yes—it's called *Fraîche Nutrition*, nothing has changed since I launched it! I love everything French and have always loved the word 'fraîche.' I used to tell my cousin that if I ever opened up an actual store, that would be what I called it.

Is running *Fraîche Nutrition* your full-time job? It is now! Up until November of 2017 it was something I did as a side hustle, but that all changed and I'm now doing it full time and absolutely loving it. Of course, I'm also a mom which takes up a chunk of time—it is the best job ever!

How has having an influencer business changed your life? It's really wonderful to have the creative freedom to make your own schedule and have zero boundaries in terms of what you can achieve: it's a real game changer. There was a lot of security and safety in working for someone else, and it was scary letting that go—I did it for 15 years. But I'm so happy that I made the leap and am still in awe on the daily at where this has taken me professionally—I'm really grateful. I have made a cookbook with my cousin Jillian and continue to grow my business, which is so much fun!

☮FRAICHENUTRITION

Tori Wesszer

est. 2014 | West Kelowna, British Columbia

⊕TEZZAMB

Tessa Barton

est. 2015 | New York City, New York

When did you start your influencer business? That is a tough question to answer since I sort of stumbled into the influencer business by accident. In my early twenties, when I was living in Utah, I started posting photos of my personal life and general interests and my posts started to gain attention. As I built up momentum and continued posting, I feel like I naturally evolved into an "influencer." I didn't really take my hobby into a career until I moved to New York City, which is when the official business side of this all took shape.

Today, my husband, Cole, and I work together, and it is definitely a team effort where we get to share creative ideas and really expand jointly. We only feel like we are just getting started, which is so exciting.

Has your blog always been called *ByTezza*? I've had a few blogs throughout the years, mostly posting about photography, music, and fashion. My current blog, *ByTezza*, is a combination of my previous blogs with a more cohesive and consistent feel to it. *ByTezza* has been my longest running blog and feels like the truest representation of myself.

What were you doing before you launched your influencer business? What inspired you to start? I was a college student getting my Bachelor of Fine Arts while playing in a touring band, writing and recording music, as well as running a photography business.

I grew up in a house of artists and entrepreneurs. Every second of spare time I found was spent creating. I loved photos, painting, making clothes, you name it my hands were in it. My mother has run a successful design business since I was a child, so watching her career was definitely an inspiration to me as I have become my own business owner.

If it was not for my loving mom and dad, I am not sure where Shop Dandy would be today.

⊙ SHOPDANDY

Danielle Downing Stackhouse

est. 2008 | Ponte Vedra, Florida

What were you doing before you launched *Shop Dandy*? Before I launched my blog, I was working for an interior design firm as an assistant. It wasn't until around 2012, a year after joining rewardStyle, that I was able to quit my day job to blog full time.

Did anyone encourage you to start blogging? There were not many people that knew I was writing a blog in 2008. It was something I kept personal, away from my friends and family, and used it as an outlet for strangers to read. It was strange to so many people that I was sharing my thoughts, photos, and life on the internet for the world to see. Blogging was more like an online journal at this time, and no one had created a guideline. I would take "selfies," mirror photos, or use a tripod if I needed a photo of myself.

Has your digital brand always been called *Shop Dandy*? My first blog name was called *Just Dandy*. My nickname has been Dandy for half my life and I wanted my blog to be

a simple extension of myself. I rebranded in 2015 to *Shop Dandy*, as a shopping destination sharing my personal style, along with the latest fashion and style trends.

Was there anyone along the way that changed the trajectory of your business? If it was not for my loving mom and dad, I am not sure where *Shop Dandy* would be today. My mom has spent countless hours taking my photos and praying for me and my business. My dad has always encouraged me to never give up, work hard, and taught me everything I know about entrepreneurship and running a business.

Do you have a motto or mission? What is it? Since day one, I have always tried to live by this mission statement: A whole healthy woman is one who is living this big, gorgeous, God-first, attractive, irresistible-to-heaven life… that draws in the lost and makes them think, 'I just want to be around her!'

est. 2015 | Los Angeles, California
Nita Mann
nextwithnita

#LTKfit

Running routines to circuit training tips,
stay motivated and moving with these
fitness, health and wellness coaches,
instructors and influencers.

gofitjo
Joanne Encarnacion
est. 2016 | San Francisco, California

fitfabfunmom
Jane Song
est. 2013 | Westlake Village, California

est. 2017 | Los Angeles, California
Britney Vest
 fittybritttty

est. 2015 | Greenville, South Carolina
Tomi Obebe
 goodtomicha

 healthyalibi
Allison Metselaar
est. 2016 | New York City, New York

Discover more workout wear and a feed full of
#LTKfit inspiration in the LIKEtoKNOW.it app.

◎JUNESIXTYFIVE

Federica Lai

est. 2014 | Montpellier, France

How did you come up with the name of your digital brand, *June Sixty-Five*? When I launched my blog, I had no idea what to call it. I wanted something original, international, and of course, something that sounded good. After some time thinking about it, I decided to call it *June Sixty-Five*, which is my mother's birthday. My mum and I are very close, so I loved this name because it meant something to me. I have never changed it.

What inspired you to launch your influencer business? My passion for fashion. All I wanted was to share it with the world! After I launched my influencer business, my entire life changed. It was the first time I did something I loved, I was very dedicated to developing it, and all my life was devoted to it.

Was there anyone along the way who had a positive influence on you and your business? Samuel, my boyfriend, helped me a lot. He was always free for photo shoots, and time after time, he became more and more influential to my business. He was there to support me and helped me to always do more!

✿THEMIDDLEPAGEBLOG

Cathy Williamson

est. 2013 | Dallas, Texas

When did you start your blog, *The Middle Page*? I started my blog in 2013, two months before being diagnosed with an aggressive form of breast cancer. I was 52 at the time that I started my blog and living in Dallas. I have just celebrated five years of my blog and five years being cancer free!

How did you come up with the name for your blog? My daughter actually came up with the name. I was trying to come up with something for "middle-aged" women and *The Middle Page* flew out of her mouth!

How has having an influencer business changed your life? I think having a blog and being an influencer has given me a purpose. After my children had all left home, I was actually scared that I would turn into

a little old lady who would eventually wither away (dramatic, I know). My blog has allowed me to meet the most wonderful women, has kept me on my toes with technology (good for my brain), and has given me self satisfaction.

What has been the most challenging thing about having an influencer business? The most challenging thing for me about having a blog is the technical side of it. I get the most frustrated with this part. If I were a high school or college age girl, I would learn coding.

What do you wish you could go back and tell yourself? Buckle your seat belt—blogging is hard work! It looks easy, but it's one of the hardest things I've ever done!

When did you start your influencer business? I started in 2009, out of high school, with a women's online brand that sold clothing, accessories, shoes, bags, wallets—everything! I loved my online shop and when I started it, I wanted more ways to advertise and get the styles that I loved out there. I then launched my blog, *Style'd Avenue*, to help style and advertise my brand. When I started my own blog, I reached out to a few of my favorite brands and styled some weekly looks. I loved blogging and running my shop 24/7. A few years later, I decided to do my blog full time. I then sold my shop and have been so happy with where I am today because I started something right out of high school.

What inspired you to launch your influencer business? I was inspired to launch my blog after having my hands in my online shop 24/7! I was so, so passionate about keeping my shop and I wanted to advertise it as much as I could! When I decided to sell the shop and launch *Style'd Avenue*, I entered into such a fun chapter and I am so happy I launched it.

What do you wish you could go back and tell yourself? I think I would tell my self to not worry as much! This is such a fun job and I'm so happy that all of my hard work turned into a successful influencer business. I love doing what I do everyday—styling, sharing, and getting inspiration from friends and other influencers all over the world!

 MEG_LEGS

Megan Williams
est. 2013 | Salt Lake City, Utah

❀ CAILAQUINN

Caila Quinn

est. 2016 | New York City, New York

What were you doing before you launched your influencer business? My life "before" feels like a different world. For three years after college, I worked in Boston in the retail software sales industry and then in marketing for a fitness startup developing pipeline reports, creating content, and staying organized—both experiences developed the skill set I still use today.

What inspired you to launch your influencer business? A hopeful romantic, I joined the Season 20 cast of ABC's *The Bachelor* looking for love. After a whirlwind experience, I immediately moved to New York City to take control of my next chapter. Instead of finding love for another person, I was gifted a platform. I cannot tell you how grateful I am for this career. I get to interact with positive and kind people and do what I love every day; be creative.

Tell us more about your blog, *With Love, Caila*, and how it all started. For me, blogging was about trial and error. Before there was *With Love, Caila*, my first blog was called *Monthful Caila*. I created the word "monthful" to describe a person who thoughtfully used their month to better themselves. Each month, I would learn a new skill and write about how it challenged me, but, in the end, the concept wasn't sustainable, so I had to toss that idea and start fresh.

The second time around, I consulted an expert to make sure it was perfect. Angela, from *Gurl Gone Social*, made my dream website come to life. Inspired by my love of letter writing, I launched *With Love, Caila* in the summer of 2016.

What is your favorite quote and what does it mean to you? One of my favorite quotes is, "Life is too short to wait to fall in love."

Whether that "falling in love" is with a job, a significant other, or yourself… life is fleeting. This quote reminds me to take advantage of every day and be grateful.

⊚ SAMANTHABELBEL
⊚ ALEXIS.BELBEL

Samantha Belbel and Alexis Belbel

est. 2015 | Dallas, Texas

When did you start your influencer business? We started our business in September 2015. We were both 24 and living in Dallas. We just kind of started posting our outfits, and with hard work, it took off! We started off photographing each other, and still do to this day!

Has your blog always been called *A Double Dose*? We have had the same blog name since we launched. Since we were launching as twins, we wanted our name to reflect that.

What were you doing before you launched *A Double Dose*? We were both working in corporate America for a large accounting firm—Samantha, in fraud technology, and Alexis, in IT auditing. We eventually transitioned careers into personal training, and then started our blog while also launching a food product.

We had followed some blogs when we were in college, but never thought we would actually become bloggers!

What inspired you to launch your influencer business? We both always had a love for fashion. After leaving our accounting jobs to pursue our passion of fitness and do personal training, we always had people inquiring about our outfits or products we used. We thought why not start posting about those things on a blog and on social media, and it took off from there!

Is there anyone along the way that changed the trajectory of your business? Having each other is probably the best thing about our job. We can bounce ideas off of each other, and always have each other's support.

⊙TAMARA

Tamara Kalinic

est. 2011 | London, United Kingdom

How did you come up with the name for your blog, *Glam & Glitter***?** I wanted it to be a little corner of the things women love, all the little luxuries, like fashion, travel, and beauty.

What were you doing before you became an influencer? At the time, I was a pharmacy student in my final year. I graduated and started working as a pharmacist—a job I thought I would be doing for the rest of my life—but little did I know that I would only practice for three years.

Is there anyone along the way that changed the trajectory of your business? My sister gave me loads of support. When quitting my job to pursue a full-time influencer career, she promised she would have my back no matter what, which really helped me relax and enjoy the journey.

What inspired you to launch your influencer business? I just genuinely wanted to meet people on the internet. When I started receiving proposals from brands, I realized that this is the moment to catch, so I quit my job and pursued blogging as a career.

What were you doing before you launched your influencer business? Before I became a content creator and influencer I was a stay-at-home mom to our two girls, Brynleigh and Brielle. I loved being a stay-at-home mom, my children have always, and will always, come first. I started modeling part time for a local boutique that also had a website and social media. I noticed I started getting a lot of questions on Instagram from people about where my clothes were from or asking where I had bought my outfit, so I started posting outfit photos on social media. From there, my following began to grow and little did I know it would one day become my career.

What inspired you to launch your influencer business? I've been inspired by so many influencers over the years. Rachel Parcell from *Pink Peonies* has always been someone I've looked up to. The way she has turned her blog into an entire clothing line and empire is so inspiring to me. She's also a young mom to two and seems to juggle it all so seamlessly! I actually had the opportunity to meet her at a blogging event we were both attending and she was just as sweet in person!

What do you wish you could go back and tell yourself? I would say, "Get ready, because your life is about to change!" I honestly never imagined what was in-store for me when I started this journey. I would also tell myself to never forget why you started blogging; to help people. Even in a small way, whether it's trying to share a daily parenting struggle I'm having or tell my followers which lip gloss is the best deal but also the best quality. At the end of the day, I'm just trying to help and connect with people.

What advice would you give to someone starting their own business? I would say to never be afraid to follow your dreams. It sounds cliché but it's so true. God has blessed us with things we are passionate about and we need to share those things with other people! Also, never be afraid to be yourself!

✿HOLLIEWDWRD

Hollie Woodward

est. 2015 | Indianapolis, Indiana

I started the blog as an online portfolio to help me find a job. I never thought it would actually be the job.

⊛HAUTEOFFTHERACK

Jennifer Palpallatoc Perrault

est. 2012 | Covington, Louisiana

When did you launch *Haute Off The Rack*? I started my blog in February of 2012. I was only 20 and still in college majoring in creative writing while trying to figure out what career path I wanted to take. I started the blog as an online portfolio to help me find a job—I never thought it could actually be the job. However, before I knew it, the blog was bringing me more opportunities than school ever did. A local Baton Rouge magazine asked me to be their fashion editor, which I did for a year while balancing school, working at a clothing boutique, and even a restaurant. A year later, the local news station asked me to start hosting on-air fashion segments.

How has *Haute Off The Rack* changed your life? Being an influencer as has changed my life tremendously and has opened doors to opportunities that I didn't even know existed, like traveling the world and snapping photos of my adventures to inspire people, while also being able to monetize my content. I'm super grateful that it allows me to provide for myself and my husband, as well as my dad, who was diagnosed with MS in April 2017 and can no longer work.

Did you have any support along the way? When I started my blog, my boyfriend at the time—who is now my husband—always remained super supportive and encouraged my crazy dreams, which he continues to do today. He actually brought me to my very first fashion week for my birthday in September 2012. I also had the help of a fellow blogger, *Brighton The Day*, who coded my whole site for me before I launched it.

To me, Bring Your Own Beauty is all about being the best version of yourself, and that's what I aspire to help women feel daily.

✷ COURTNEY_SHIELDS

Courtney Shields

est. 2014 | Austin, Texas

What year did you start *Bring Your Own Beauty*? I started my blog, *Bring Your Own Beauty*, in January of 2014. I was 26 at the time and living in Dallas with my now-husband, Alex, who was playing linebacker for the Dallas Cowboys!

What were you doing before you launched your influencer business? I was actually doing music full time when I started my blog. I had recently graduated from Berklee College of Music and was writing songs, playing shows, and teaching guitar and piano to kids during the week.

What inspired you to launch your influencer business? I found myself getting the same frantic text messages and calls from friends in retail stores, "I'm in this store and I need a primer for oily skin, what do I buy?" After years of receiving similar texts, I was having a conversation with my brother at our family's cottage in Vermont. I remember telling him how I wished I was able to help more than just the people currently closest to me. He looked at me and said, "Why don't you start a blog?" The rest is history as they say!

Has your blog always been called *Bring Your Own Beauty*? My blog has always been called *Bring Your Own Beauty*. When I first started, I often just called it *BYOBeauty*, but now I either say *Bring Your Own Beauty* or BYOB! My husband will tell you that he came up with the name while drinking a beer on the couch one day. He looked at me and said, "What about BYOB?!" We expanded from there. I really wanted a name that would embody a lifestyle and a mindset. To me, *Bring Your Own Beauty* is all about being the best version of yourself, and that's what I aspire to help women feel daily.

What inspired you to launch an influencer business? My uncles had a really successful online business and would always pitch me ideas. Right out of college I created an SEO website and had hopes to help small businesses with their online presence. At the same time, I was going through a breakup and decided I needed change. I moved to San Francisco and the blog was born. Funny enough, the breakup that inspired the move, which inspired the blog, was with my now husband and business partner.

Has your blog always been called *Crystalin Marie*? I started my blog when I moved to San Francisco and *In the City with Crystalin* seemed like the perfect title. Two years into blogging, I moved back to my hometown and figured my blog needed a new name. I wanted something that would be forever constant and reflect who I was, so *Crystalin Marie* was born. I wanted to keep my name in the title because I knew people would remember it. It's unique and different!

What has been the most challenging thing about being an influencer? There's never enough time and there's always something to do. Social media doesn't stop, so it's hard to know when to close your laptop and turn your phone off. It's difficult to have work/life balance. As a new mom, I'm really learning that time is precious.

How has having an influencer business changed your life? Where do I begin? It has given me and my family the freedom to live life the way we always dreamed. I knew from the very beginning that I wanted to have something of my own; to work for myself. I never in a million years thought it would come in the form of influencing and sharing my passions with the world. Our influencer business has allowed my husband, Mike, to leave his job to help grow *Crystalin Marie*. It has allowed us to raise a family from home, which was something we always dreamed about, and it's also allowed us to buy our first home.

I never in a million years thought it would come in the form of influencing and sharing my passions with the world.

❂ CRYSTALINMARIE

Crystalin Da Silva

est. 2010 | Portland, Oregon

PHOTOGRAPHY CREDITS

Inside Front Cover *(top : left to right)* Darian Esser, Vanessa Chavez, Lucy Hernandez, *(middle : left to right)* Ariel Rini, Kendi Skeen, Erin Broege, *(bottom : left to right)* Mary Hafner, Mary Hafner | **Opposite Inside Front Cover** *(top : left to right)* Novelyn Parent, Ashley McGrath, *(middle : left to right)* Shelly Johnson, Rebecca Rosen Patton, Courtney Wyse, *(bottom : left to right)* Tandya Stewart, Dede Raad, Jasmine Ricks | **Opposite Title Page** *(top : left to right)* Lauren Armellini, Nina Schwichtenberg, *(middle : left to right)* Yash Singh, Emily Herren, Melissa Cole, *(bottom : left to right)* Rebecca Rosen Patton, Stella Eneanya, Jaime Shrayber | **6** : Mindy Byrd | **9** *(top : left to right)* Amber Venz Box, Lauren Logan, *(bottom : left to right)* Scot Redman, Amber Venz Box | **10 and 11** *(all images)* Jessica Steddom | **12** : Michael Hillyard | **13** *(left to right)* Meghan Savage, Michael Hillyard | **14 and 15** *(all images)* Lauren Kay Sims | **16** *(top left)* Sassy Red Lipstick, *(bottom left)* Alexis Exstrom, *(right)* Sassy Red Lipstick | **19** *(all images)* Rebecca Smith | **21** : Erica Key | **22** *(top : left to right)* Jessi Afshin, Divina Stennfeld, *(bottom : left and right)* Jessi Afshin | **24** : *(all images)* Alaina Kaczmarski and Danielle Moss | **27** : *(all images)* Robert Swanson | **29** *(all images)* Blair Staky | **30** *(top : left and right)* Narci Dreffs, *(bottom : left and right)* Chris Sims | **32 and 33** *(all images)* Leonie Hanne | **34 and 35** *(all images)* Les Andrew | **36 and 37** *(all images)* Louise Roe | **38** *(all images)* Randi Garrett | **41** *(left)* Angie Garcia, *(top and bottom right)* Ailee Petrovic | **42 and 43** *(all images)* Jessica Wang | **44** *(left)* Angie Garcia, *(right)* Kate Padgitt | **45** *(left)* Angie Garcia, *(right)* Claire Pedregon | **46** *(all images)* Erika Fox | **48 and 49** *(all images)* John Philp Thompson III | **51** *(all images)* Bri Costello | **52** : Samantha Wennerstrom | **53** *(left)* Jacqueline Pilar, *(right)* Samantha Wennerstrom | **54 and 55** *(all images)* Carla Covington | **56** *(all images)* Melanie Elturk | **58 and 59** *(all images)* Zabrina Hancock | **60** *(top right)* Shannon Willardson, *(top right : profile image)* Alexis Exstrom, *(bottom left)* Miriam Gin, *(bottom right)* Laura Wills | **61** *(top left)* Tara Gibson, *(top right)* Kate Blue, *(bottom left)* Shay Sweeney, *(bottom left : profile image)* Ahmad Sweeney | **63** : Shana Draugelis | **64 and 65** *(all images)* Kendall Kremer | **67** *(all images)* John Smith | **68 and 69** *(all images)* Craig S. Mackay | **71** : Juli Bauer Roth | **72** *(all images)* Kayla Seah | **74** : Christian Barnes | **76** *(all images)* Jennifer Lake | **78** : Alyssa Ence | **79** *(top left to right)* Becki Owens, Lindsay Salazar, *(bottom left to right)* Ryan Garvin | **81** : Dave Awasthi | **82** *(all images)* Kelly Larkin | **84** : Ranti Onayemi | **86 and 87** *(all images)* Anush Mohan | **88 and 89** *(all images)* Sandi Johnson and Shalia Ashcraft | **90** *(all images)* Juliet Angus | **91** : Rebecca Spencer | **92** *(all images)* Nastia Liukin | **94 and 97** *(all images)* Paige Sovic | **98 and 99** *(all images)* Liz Adams | **100** *(top left)* Rebecca Patton, *(bottom left and right)* Lauren Johnson | **103** *(all images)* Sona Gasparian | **104 and 105** *(all images)* Uduak Bassey | **106** : Jamie Hodge | **107** *(all images)* Monika Hibbs | **109** *(all images)* Jen Adams | **110 and 111** *(all images)* Lauren Murphy | **112** *(top right)* Erin Wheeler, *(bottom left)* Anita Yokota, *(bottom right)* Tamara Anka | **113** *(top left)* Jennifer Holmes, *(top right)* Kelley Nan Lopez, *(bottom left)* Julia and Chris Marcum | **114** : Kemper Baugh | **115** *(top left to right)* Kemper Baugh, Jordan Baugh, *(bottom left to right)* Jordan Baugh, Kemper Baugh | **116** *(all images)* Emily Ann Gemma | **119** *(all images)* Anh S. | **120 and 121** *(all images)* Cara Irwin | **122 and 123** *(all images)* Tom McGovern | **124** *(all images)* Jillian Harris | **126** : Eduardo Bravin | **128 and 129** *(all images)* Mackenzie Horan Beuttenmuller | **130 and 131** *(all images)* Brittany Robertson | **132 and 133** *(all images)* Chelsae Anne | **134 and 135** *(all images)* Courtney Kerr | **136 and 137** *(all images)* Kamikka McCoy | **139** *(top left and right)* Anthony Pulsifer, *(bottom left)* Anthony Pulsifer, *(bottom right)* Terri Roberts | **140** *(all images)* Mary Hafner | **143** *(all images)* Daphné Moreau | **144** *(all images)* Brittany Hayes | **145** : Paige Ewing | **146 and 147** *(all images)* Erica Hoida | **148 and 149** *(all images)* Brooke Tredway and Meggan Bowlsby | **150** *(all images)* Jean Wang | **152** : Felicia Lasala | **153** *(top left and right)* Felicia Lasala, *(bottom left)* Felicia Lasala, *(bottom right)* Shalice Noel | **154** *(all images)* Olivia Watson | **155** *(top left)* Anna Szczekutowicz, *(top right)* Olivia Watson | **156** (top left) Krystal Faircloth, (bottom left and right) Lainey Reed | **159** (all images) Allen Daniel Dubnikov | **160 and 161** (all images) Jennifer Prock | **163** *(all images)* Christine Andrew | **164** *(top right)* Erica Matthews, *(bottom left)* Hailey and Kailey Nouis, *(bottom right)* Lindsey Regan Thorne | **165** *(top left)* Sona Gasparian, *(top right)* Angie Garcia, *(bottom left)* Andrea De Silva | **166** *(all images)* Jessica Ricks | **168 and 169** *(all images)* Anna Sandul | **170 and 171** *(all images)* Olia Majd | **172** *(top left)* Paulo Piexoto, *(top right)* Rhelden Nogueira | **173** : Clecio R. B. Dourado | **174** *(top)* Kelly Nemeth, *(bottom left)* Liz Joy, *(bottom right)* Shaye Babb | **176** *(all images)* Sabrina Tan | **178** : Emily Men | **180** : Grace Wainwright | **181** *(top left)* Jordan M. White, *(top right)* Erin Trimble | **182 and 183** *(all images)* Ashley Robertson | **184 and 185** *(all images)* Steph Sterjovski Jolly | **186** *(top)* Russell Heeter, *(bottom left)* Tamara Waterston, *(bottom right)* Kayleigh Alberts | **189** *(all images)* Jeff Dashley | **190 and 191** *(all images)* Audrie Sue Dollins | **192** *(top left to right)* Victoria Elizabeth Metaxas, Kaylee Labor, *(bottom left to right)* Victoria Elizabeth Metaxas, Alyson Haley | **194 and 195** *(all images)* Rebecca Patton | **196** *(all images)* Aylin G | **198** *(all images)* Lauren Price | **200 and 201** *(all images)* Kris Jarrett | **202** *(all images)* Ashley Burns | **204** *(all images)* Tori Wesszer | **206 and 207** *(all images)* Tessa Barton | **208 and 209** *(all images)* Danielle Downing Stackhouse | **210** *(top right)* Nita Mann, *(bottom left)* Joanne Encarnacion, *(bottom right)* Jane Song | **211** *(top left)* Britney Vest, *(top right)* Chelsey Ashford, *(bottom left)* Allison Metselaar, *(bottom left : profile image)* Rafe Masters | **212 and 213** *(all images)* Federica Lai | **214 and 215** *(all images)* Mary Hafner | **217** *(all images)* Megan Williams | **218** *(all images)* Caila Quinn | **220 and 221** *(all images)* Alexis and Samantha Belbel | **222 and 223** *(all images)* Tamara Kalinic | **225** *(all images)* Jeremy Johnson | **226** *(all images)* Kristen Waguespack | **227** *(top left)* Lainey Reed, *(top right)* Kristen Waguespack | **228** *(all images)* Alex Albright | **230** *(all images)* Crystalin Da Silva | **Opposite Photography Credits** *(top : left to right)* Shannon Righetti, Jaclyn Ram, *(middle : left to right)* Anisa Sojka, Jennifer Mandriota, Candace Hampton, *(bottom : left to right)* Camilla Thurman, Mary Hafner, Debra Kiriewsky | **Opposite Inside Back Cover** *(top : left to right)* Adelina Perrin, Carissa Miller, SimplyJaserah, *(middle : left to right)* Merritt Beck, Megan Ardoin, Brittany Sjogren, *(bottom : left to right)* Christine Kong, Sarah Ellis and Philippa Ross | **Inside Back Cover** *(top : left to right)* Sinead Crowe, Sasa Zoe, *(middle : left to right)* Emily Roberts, Katie Manwaring, Carolina Hellal Jaramillo, *(bottom : left to right)* Jennifer Reed, Erin Busbee, Francis L. Baker IV

wannabefashionblogger

myviewinheels

anisasojka

mrscasual

thebeautybeau

navygraceblog

themilleraffect

sunsetsandstilettos

thecharmingolive

ccandmikecreative

simplyjaserah

merrittbeck

honeywerehome

loverlygrey

dailykongfidence

wearetwinset